J. E. H. MacDonald

Paul Duval

THE TANGLED GARDEN

CEREBRUS/PRENTICE-HALL

Foreword

I first met J.E.H.MacDonald at the Arts and Letters Club in 1920. At that time several of the Group of Seven would meet for lunch and usually Jim would be there. As a young artist I was eager to hear their conversation about art, but rarely did Jim discuss painting, he was so interested in so many different things that he wished to talk about.

In the 58 years since I first met him, my admiration and respect for this gentle, sincere man and his work has steadily increased. He was the complete artist in everything he did, never doing anything shoddy because of insufficient time or payment. He had a high standard and maintained it in everything. As much effort went into the Christmas decorations for the Arts and Letters Club as he would expend for an important painting.

As a designer he was to my mind one of the best. He had no formula either in designing or painting. Each piece of work was approached in a manner appropriate to the subject. This attitude and his marvellous sense of design kept him from ever repeating a composition.

In the twelve years I knew Jim, I very seldom saw him upset; it was only when some stupid criticism appeared in the art columns, that he would reply with a biting and thoughtful answer, and then always with a great sense of humour.

I learned much from Jim; from his attitude toward painting, from his kindly criticism, but most of all from the man himself. I will always remember working on a mural for him. He had made the small sketches and because of ill health and an early completion date, he asked if I would do the large work. I completed it and not until then did he come to see how I was getting along. He came into the room and stood looking at it for some time and remarked that I had done a good job, but asked almost apologetically would I mind if he just added a few touches. I watched him at work and was amazed how his keen eye had spotted the flaws.

I am very happy to see this handsome book produced about my old friend's work. No Canadian artist deserves it more. I only hope that it will inspire young painters to emulate the approach MacDonald had to painting–to be his own man!

A.J.Casson, LLD., O.S.A., R.C.A.
Toronto

Algoma Waterfall, 1920

Introduction

In the formative years of the first nationalist movement in Canadian Art no one contributed more both spiritually and artistically than James Edward Hervey MacDonald. In the years since his death, two slight books with printings of a few hundred copies have appeared.

This volume, appropriately named for one of his most criticized and paradoxically most admired paintings, is a belated celebration of the life and works of a great Canadian painter.

Years of struggle and deprivation concluded only by death, with applause after the curtain has dropped are the elements of the stereotyped scenario for an artist's life. MacDonald fits this classic mirthless casting.

In an era when one's innermost thoughts and feelings were frequently poured into letters and diaries, MacDonald expressed his ardour for an art form strongly identified with our nation and its boundless grandeur. Even more fervently he asked on behalf of his fellow artists that Canadians recognize the character of their native land and the enthusiasm and sincerity the little band of painters had for extracting its essence.

Fortunately many of these personal notes have survived and the author has used them to the fullest to create an intimacy with the artist through his own words.

As a journal it traces MacDonald's travels from Nova Scotian shores to the Rockies and focuses on the zenith of his painterly powers in the rugged majesty of Algoma's wilderness. Here the impasto from a brush often loaded with pure colour assaulted the panel with absolute sureness.

The magnificent array of his works in this book belies the biographical portrait of a man of less than robust health whose image is often one verging on frailty. Ranging from his earliest Barbizon influenced paintings which give no hint of the vibrant pictorial lode he was to extract later from the northern winds, the retrospective selection provides a sumptuous visual feast.

The sheer power in controlled explosions of colour and design formed his wilderness panels and canvases describing a rarely equalled vision of that awesome land.

Robert McMichael, C.M., D. Litt.
Kleinburg, Ontario

Algoma Trees, 1920

Preface

I am deeply indebted to Thoreau MacDonald, artist, naturalist and son of J.E.H.MacDonald for invaluable assistance in the preparation of this book. During an acquaintance spanning more than twenty years, I have been a regular beneficiary of Thoreau's keen devotion to his father's achievements, and to his careful preservation of family documents. I have had free access to his father's lifelong correspondence. Since I agree with J.E.H.MacDonald's statement that "documents are the best material *if written at the time*," his letters are the basis for the facts in this book. In many cases, these are corrections of material which has appeared in public gallery catalogues.

I wish to express my appreciation to the painters, A.J.Casson and Carl Schaefer, who were closely acquainted with MacDonald, to Jack MacDonald and to Hunter Bishop, librarian of the Arts and Letters Club, Toronto. I also would like to make mention of the public galleries and private collectors who put their work so readily at my disposal. In this connection, close cooperation has been given by Alice Armstrong of the National Gallery of Canada, Maia-Mari Sutnik of the Art Gallery of Ontario, Keith Courtney of the Art Gallery of Hamilton, Robert McMichael, Jim Hubbard, and Denis Jones of the McMichael Canadian Collection, the staff of the London Art Gallery and the staff of the Saskatoon Gallery and Conservatory.

Paul Duval,
The Studio Building, Toronto,
July 9, 1978

Mount Lefroy, 1932

Contents

The Early Years

James Edward Hervey MacDonald is an authentic hero of Canadian art. A philosophical and gentle man, his landscapes are among the most powerful of the famed Group of Seven. With Lawren Harris, he was the moving spirit behind that band of artists. He led the future Group members in their early battles against neglect and opposition. He was an eloquent spokesman, an accomplished poet, and a natural teacher, eager to share his enthusiasm, knowledge and experience. He was a friend and mentor of Tom Thomson, and the biggest single influence upon that painter. MacDonald demanded relentless perfection in art and craft from a body that was often beleaguered by ill-health throughout his fifty-nine, frequently debt-ridden, years. His life was one of immense courage and creative dedication.

It would be difficult to find a more truly Canadian artist than J.E.H.MacDonald. Although born in England, his loyalties and career were intimately bound up with Canada. He was the only original member of the Group of Seven whose art training was exclusively taken in this country. Lismer, Varley and Carmichael all studied in Antwerp, Jackson in Paris, Harris in Munich and Johnston in Philadelphia.

MacDonald was not only one of Canada's greatest artists, but by far the most steeped in the New World. His ancestors on his father's side were North American for several hundred years. They did not come over on the *Mayflower*, but did arrive a few vessels later, on board the *Arabella*, and generations later made their way north to Quebec as United Empire Loyalists.

MacDonald's grandfather served as a non-commissioned officer in the Canadian Army, first at Halifax and St. John, Quebec, and later at Fort York in Toronto. About 1860, he was posted to Fort Garry, via Hudson Bay, and during the difficult journey his daughter, Marischa, froze to death. J.E.H.MacDonald's father, William Henry, who had been born in the St. John barracks in 1852, survived the trip and completed his schooling, which had begun in Toronto, in a Jesuit Mission School at Fort Garry. Although he remained an Anglican, William Henry retained some sympathy for the Catholic spirit. When he visited Durham, England, as a young man, he married a young Catholic girl, Margaret Usher, and remained in the area for more than fifteen years. In the nearby village of New Elvet, on May 12, 1873, J.E.H.MacDonald, their first child, was born. Two sisters, Bertha and Daisy, and a brother, William, came later.

As a child, Jamie MacDonald came to know the hilly country of Durham intimately. He was not a strong child, but he later claimed that the countryside in which he grew up and played had a strong effect upon that affection for rugged landscape which eventually led him to his Algoma and mountain masterpieces. He attended the local Model School in Durham, but

Nova Scotia, 1898

Epping Forest, c 1905

spent his very earliest years in the nearby town of Kirkby Stephen where he caught small trout and sailed model sailboats on the River Wear. He went on these expeditions with an older boy from whom he acquired that first taste for books which led to a lifetime devotion to literature.

"I was about five years old, and he was about sixteen," MacDonald recalled later, "and I followed him always with reverence. After an afternoon of sailing ships, we'd come home and he'd read *Robinson Crusoe* to me. I've read the book often since then, but I've never been so delighted with it as I was then."

Jamie MacDonald was a good student, even a bookworm. He won a copy of Lamb's *Tales From Shakespeare* as a school prize when he was eleven. "I remember," he wrote to his future wife, Joan Lavis, "how I walked home on the day I got it – with some schoolmates – looking at the pictures all the way. I liked it very much, and I'm grateful to it because it opened the way to Shakespeare himself. …I must have read far more than I can remember, because I was continually sitting poring over books. I wasn't a strong enough boy to succeed in games, so I spent much time in reading, often sitting on the doorstep I remember, with one of the babies, Bertha or Daisy, in one arm, and holding a book with the other hand."

It is interesting, if fruitless, to conjecture where MacDonald's passion may have led him if he had been able to continue his education, instead of starting to work as a teen-ager. His family was not well-to-do, and when his father returned to Canada and settled in Hamilton in Jamie's fourteenth year, the boy was immediately apprenticed to a lithographing company. That move sealed his future irrevocably.

"For the first four years in Canada," he wrote later, "I read very little. I had to go to work during the day and to art school at night, and most of my leisure time was spent out of doors." The night classes he attended during the first three Canadian years were at the Hamilton Art School, and it is possible that one of his teachers there was Arthur Heming, a future friend.

That Hamilton art apprenticeship which was to lead to future greatness ended when MacDonald's family moved to Toronto when he was seventeen. In Toronto, he first obtained a job for a few years at the Toronto Lithographing Company, before moving to Grip Limited, a leading firm of designers and engravers. He also reacquired the habit of reading. He spent all his pocket money on books. "I was a hermit in those days," he wrote a friend. "Though I had companions, I had no friends, except these speaking spirits of books. I might have read less and that more carefully, but I had no one to guide me in this, so I just read whatever came to me." What came to him from the book stores along Yonge Street included Plato, Lowell, Cook's Voyages, Montaigne, Carlyle, Goethe, Cicero and Burns.

Robert Burns particularly appealed to the young apprentice designer, and the Scottish poet was to remain his lifetime favourite, along with Walt Whitman. "How well I remember buying my first copy of Burns. How I hastened from Yonge Street to those quiet residential streets around the Normal School, and carefully drew the little book from my pocket, and there snatched little glimpses of it, all the rest of the way home. I read it over and over and carried it with me always. It was my first conscious listening to the music that is all about us, and it opened my ears. …In my walks in the woods I had Burns with me, and many a Sunday morn have he and I spent together in Rosedale."

Burns had his creative consequences upon the young and romantic MacDonald. "Soon I began to try writing, for I got into that condition which so often caused Burns to write, I fell in love no less. On the flat above ours a number of young girls were employed. I used to see them going into work in the morning and coming out at night, and I soon learned to look on one of them with great interest. She was a little, gentle-looking, sweet-faced girl. I never got to know her, but I liked her very much, and my youthful heart found expression in one or two Scottish songs. They were the first things I ever wrote, so Robert Burns and that young lady are partially responsible for other sins of that kind I have committed since."

In his solitary life, the slim, red-headed MacDonald next discovered John Ruskin, and it was that English writer who led him to begin drawing the flowers and foliage that began to fill his sketch books. [This interest was later reinforced by the brilliant flower studies by painter Robert Holmes.] But the young artist was still undirected in his life's ambitions. "I wasted my time in foolish amusements," he later confessed. "I had no definite aim; if I got through the work of the day easily and spent the evening pleasantly I was satisfied."

Early in 1896, MacDonald met a new employee of Grip Limited, Lewis Smith. Smith worked only briefly at Grip, but he and MacDonald became fast friends and often sketched together. Later in 1896, MacDonald visited his friend's home in Nova Scotia, and returned there in 1898, trips which would be repeated into the 1920s. This relationship was crucial to MacDonald. "For the first time since my boyhood I had a friend," he wrote to Joan Lavis on New Years, 1898. "Many companions I had all along, but Lewis was different. Then, for a little while, he left me, and I missed him much. ...I had such a feeling of solitude that I wrote to Lewis telling him how strongly I wished to have some good girl friend. The next letter brought me news of your goodwill toward me, and I have rejoiced since then in the possession of a perfect friend."

That perfect friend, Harriet Joan Lavis, was attending McMaster University, then located in Toronto. A tall, dark, brown-eyed girl, she had been born in the town of Hampton, near Oshawa, Ontario. Her father, John Rich Lavis, was a carriage builder, a Huguenot from the Channel Island of Sark. Young Joan was a dedicated Christian Scientist from girlhood, and although she never seems to have attempted to convert MacDonald from his non-denominational Christianity, she remained a Scientist throughout her life. [When J.E.H. was buried, it was with a Christian Science service.] The couple did share an almost religious dedication to the American author and naturalist, Henry David Thoreau.

The years of quiet courtship between the couple resulted in a correspondence that revealed much about MacDonald as a young man. He was clearly not only a loner, apart from his close attachment to Joan Lavis and Lewis Smith, but often found his day-to-day life a little boring. "I've passed this week in the same old way," he wrote about Grip Limited in December, 1896, "in the same old place, with my nose down to the same old work. There is very little variation in the shop life."

MacDonald's early letters reveal much about the character of some commercial art at the time. "Let me tell you," he wrote in April, 1897, "about my day's work. The job I had was typical of much in our modern business methods. It was a label for a patent medicine – 'Dr. Clarke's Stomach and Liver Tonic' – made by Imperial Medicine Co. of Toronto. These gentlemen thought that a picture of Dr. Clarke would look well on the label – give it a dignity and certain interest, etc. 'Very well, have you a picture of the Dr.?' They hadn't, as the gentleman is an entirely imaginary person, and so to supply their want we looked through a number of English illustrated papers containing small portraits of public men – M.P.s, authors, men of science – and choosing one of a portly gentleman, with side whiskers, a bald head, and a ponderous kind of air, we stuck him on the label, and he'll go out before all the world as the inventor of this wonderful medicine!"

MacDonald was to work for Grip Limited, as an employee and free-lancer, for nearly twenty years, and the character of his work and his attitude towards his employment there improved greatly with time. MacDonald's finest work as a designer was unsurpassed at that time. He owed much of his skill to the example of Robert Holmes, who taught at the Central Ontario School of Art and Design, and designed many of the ornate covers for the remarkable Art Students League calendars of the late 'nineties. Holmes was a diligent student of the work of William Morris and Walter Crane, and his enthusiasm for these artists rubbed off on his younger colleague. MacDonald's fondness for design, painting and poetry ran in tandem for most of his life, and as eventual head designer of Grip Limited, he strongly influenced many younger artists in these realms.

In March 1899, MacDonald wrote in high spirits to Lewis Smith in Nova Scotia: "I do hope that you will get to Toronto this year, for a special reason. I will have a house of my own to invite you to. For, my friend Lewis, the friendship which you were the visible means of beginning is now to pass into a higher stage. Joan and I are to be married this Spring. We expect the day to be my birthday, May 12."

And so the two were married on MacDonald's twenty-sixth birthday in Toronto's west end Swansea district at a small church overlooking High Park. It was a very small wedding, and the guests included fellow artists Norman Price, William Wallace and Archie Martin, who were

Untitled Sketch

soon to play an important role in MacDonald's future. The couple honeymooned for several days at Bronte, Ontario, where MacDonald had previously gone to sketch several times. Upon their return, MacDonald left his parents' home at 113 Bellwoods Avenue and rented a small cottage at 572 Quebec Avenue, near High Park. Two years later, he designed and had built a six-room cream stucco house of his own at 475 Quebec Avenue [later renumbered 105]. A son, Thoreau, the only child, was born there on April 21, 1901. The three became an extremely close-knit family. MacDonald was a very domestic man, devoted to his home, and whenever he was away kept in constant contact through letters full of affection, diverting observations and entertaining trivia. At Quebec Avenue, Joan MacDonald would play the organ, sometimes with the vocal accompaniment of friends, or J.E.H. would read aloud, a favourite practice he continued through his lifetime. At the time of his marriage, he was making twelve dollars a week at Grip Limited.

As a painter, MacDonald was a relatively slow starter. In 1898, when he was twenty-five, he was still taking Saturday afternoon lessons at the Central Ontario School of Art and Design under George A.Reid. MacDonald couldn't have been more fortunate in his teacher. Although only thirteen years older than MacDonald, Reid was already a consummately trained artist and instructor. Born in Wingham, Ontario, he had spent three years at the Pennsylvania Academy in Philadelphia under the great Thomas Eakins and a year in Paris with Benjamin Constant at the Julian Academy and later at the Colarossi Academy.

At the time he began teaching with the Central Ontario School in 1890, Reid, with his advanced foreign training, was looked upon by most of his Toronto colleagues as a modernist, or "eliminator", as the popular phrase was then. Reid's bold brush strokes and tonal simplification shocked most of the leading Toronto painters of the period whose styles leaned to careful glazes, delicate brushwork and a highly meticulous technique. Lucius O'Brien, the first President of the Royal Canadian Academy, was quoted as saying: "Reid is one of the eliminators. He could easily ruin Canadian art; but there's one thing, no one will ever want to buy his pictures." Reid went on to become Principal of the Ontario College of Art, successor to the Central Ontario School of Art and Design, and a potent influence on two generations of Canadian painters and designers.

There is no doubt that George Reid had a strong early influence upon J.E.H.MacDonald. The younger artist's letters of the 1890s include many references to Reid, particularly when he was writing to Lewis Smith in Nova Scotia. "Mr. Reid's class began work early in January," he wrote on January 29, 1898. "We have had four lessons so far. I like the work immensely, and I am going forward, I think. I am weak in drawing, but according to Mr. Reid, I put my 'notes' of colour true. Perhaps I would do better in landscape than in figure, tho', of course, poor drawing is detrimental to either. Mr. Reid is a good teacher, careful, ample in explanation, ready to demonstrate anything he says, with his brush. I see now the reason of the importance given to 'technique' by artists. I used to think it a fanciful fad of theirs. Attending the class has made me more on the alert for colour than I used to be. And if one can *see* colour he'll soon learn how to mix it and put it on canvas." A little later he wrote, "Mr. Reid gave me a good criticism today, one that made me see something. He did something he never did before – painted in a piece of work and then scraped it out with the palette knife. I'd like very much to see some of his early work. I'm sure it would help to contradict my discouragement."

"I'm still attending the Saturday morning classes, Lewis," he wrote in the following year, "and am making *some* progress, of course. I can produce a study that has some semblance to the model. But I'm looking forward to greater improvement by outdoor work in the summer. Truly the craft is hard to learn, especially when one gives only one afternoon to the practice of it. But it is good to give that much, and if the little time is rightly used, more time will come. We are bound to express ourselves and that is all we want to do."

The association between the two men that began as a teacher-student relationship was maintained over the years. MacDonald would one day succeed Reid as principal of the Ontario College of Art, and Reid would paint a portrait of him for that institution.

For most of his early outdoor sketching, MacDonald went to the Humber River and nearby High Park. High Park was the artist's Walden. Close by his home on Quebec Avenue, it offered him hundreds of acres of woods, fields and water. "There are dozens of pictures in High Park now coming home," he recorded in the 'nineties. "Wherever I look the landscape took the most beautiful composition and colour." He painted High Park in many weathers and perspectives. He used the park as a theme for oil sketches as small as a hand and for large, major canvases over a period of more than a decade. As a painter, it was for him what Hampstead Heath had been for Constable. Most of all, it was a place that pleased his love of nature and renewed his poetic soul.

In his spare moments, MacDonald was always drawing with pencil, in small, pocket-sized sketch books. In a typical 1896 sketch book there are studies of flowers, hands, figures and landscapes of the Kennedy Farm which was located on the north side of Bloor Street across from High Park. A 1900 sketch book features drawings of the artist's two pets, a dog "Jock", and a cat "Nicolenka", poppies, a skunk cabbage and a dead sparrow, which he took home to draw after it had been thrown into an open streetcar in which he was riding. Sky studies predominate in the pages of his books, followed by scenery of the Humber River. Most of these early drawings are analytical learning exercises. Some of them, despite their seriousness, have great charm, and occasionally the artist sweeps an area with a coloured wash or two.

During the 1890s, MacDonald came to know a number of local artists who had formed a group called the Toronto Art Students League. The League's aim was similar to that of the later Group of Seven, to search out and portray subjects peculiar to Canadian life and landscape. The last spike of the Canadian Pacific Railway had been driven the year before the Art Students League was founded in 1886, and a sense of nationalism was high in the land. The League's moving spirit was designer A.H.Howard, who was enthusiastically joined by fellow local artists Robert Holmes, Charles W.Manly, J.D.Kelly, O.R.Hughes and W.W.Alexander. Their weekly sketching and discussion sessions at 56 King Street in downtown Toronto were soon joined by such younger painters as Fred H.Brigden, C.W.Jefferys, W.J.Thomson, David F.Thomson and Mary Wrinch.

The members of the Toronto Art Students League sketched outdoors together, as well as in the studio. They travelled to rural locations around the city and, in the process, produced some of the finest pen and pencil drawings of landscape ever done in Canada. There was a fresh sparkle and vigour to their best efforts, and they were almost all skilled in that most difficult medium – pen drawing. From 1893 to 1904, many of these drawings were collected in annual Art League calendars, which formed a rich record of the state of graphic art in the country at the time.

MacDonald's personal recognition of the major role played by Art League members and their contemporaries in laying the foundations of a native Canadian art was vigorously spelled out in a letter written [but never sent] to Fred B.Housser [December 10, 1926], after the publication of the latter's "A Canadian Art Movement". MacDonald was critical of what he thought was the book's overemphasis on the contribution of Grip Limited artists [many of them future members of the Group of Seven] toward a Canadian School of painting. "I realize in reading over the book that it is difficult to give things their proper order and sequence. It seems to me that the stage is not properly set at the beginning. Things begin too definitely in Grip Co. Men like Reid, Jefferys and Fred Brigden, Arthur Goode, Conacher, Plaskett and others had their place as pioneers and encouragers. The Art League and its annual publication, the Graphic Arts Club with its Canadian evenings [the fellows all singing Sid Howard's canoe songs ranged like canoe-men on the benches]. The visiting evenings we used to have at different artists' studios, to make half-hour compositions on Canadian subjects. There was a great stirring of *Canadian* ideals. Old

Cruikshank, for instance, with his 'Breaking the Road' was a more Canadian influence among us than any Krieghoff, and Reid's City Hall decorations meant much to us. Dave Thomson's name also occurs to me as one of our local heroes. His pen drawings in the Art League Calendar, and his watercolours of Algonquin Park and Scarboro Bluffs were landmarks to us."

The influence of the Toronto Art Students League upon MacDonald personally can hardly be exaggerated. In the League he could share his efforts, criticism and social life with his fellows. The importance of constant drawing espoused by the League agreed with his diligent nature. The League's motto was *Nulla Dies Sine Linea* [Not a Day Without A Line], and this unquestionably appealed to a young artist who had already been assiduously sketching everything in sight for some years. The concision and expressiveness of his draftsmanship grew dramatically during his League association.

The Art Students League decided the future direction of his life in a very immediate way. Three of his League colleagues, all commercial artists, left Toronto for London, England, where they established the Carlton Studio Designers and Illustrators firm at 180 Fleet Street. The group, composed of Archie A.Martin, William T.Wallace and Norman M.Price, soon flourished in their new environment, with their English associate, A.A.Turbayne. Late in 1903, they invited MacDonald to join them as a designer, and in December of that year, he reluctantly left his family and sailed for London.

It took MacDonald a while to adjust to the busy new milieu of London. Uprooted from his familiar Toronto surroundings, he buried his initial melancholy with long hours at the Carlton Studio, and long walks in the outskirts of the city. For a weekly wage of five pounds and eight shillings, he worked Tuesdays and Thursdays from nine until six and on Mondays, Wednesdays and Fridays from nine a.m. until nine p.m. But he found the work congenial and reported that: "I put in the day, doing, generally speaking, nicer work than at Grip. It also gives me satisfaction to know that I am doing something towards paying off our indebtedness."

On weekends MacDonald did his sightseeing, leaving on long forays from the top floor room that he shared with Norman Price at a four storey boarding house in North Central London called "Adrian House". He made regular visits to the British Museum, and the National and Tate Galleries. He also discovered Hampstead Heath: "Last Tuesday I went out to Hampstead Heath. It is a beautiful place, just as wild as High Park over a great part of it, reminding me very strongly of High Park with its oaks and rolling hills."

But he missed the closeness of domesticity. "I am just home from work a little while," he wrote home on January 15, 1904. "Now the bell of St. Paul's which you write about is chiming a quarter to eleven. So you see I ought to be creeping into bed. But I know you like to think of me writing you, however little, and perhaps at this very moment [about seven o'clock Friday night with you] you are writing to me. Dear lassie, I do miss you. As long as I am working, I don't long to see you particularly, any more that I would if I were at Grip. But, coming home and seeing the stars and the streets – everything so much like Toronto, it seems as though you might be waiting for me at home, and yet I cannot *see you* there. And, tonight, in particular, it seemed as though you ought to be here."

After almost a year, MacDonald returned to Toronto to pick up his wife and child for a return trip to London. They now lived in a flat at Loughton on the edge of Epping Forest, just northeast of London. The correspondence between the artist and his wife continued because of frequent separations when Joan MacDonald would travel with Thoreau to places like Torquay and Wallington, Surrey, to bolster her health. From London, J.E.H. would report to her about sketching trips or his regular visits to the city's galleries. On July 15, 1906, he informed her: "I went to South Kensington to look at the De Wint watercolours, but, of course, to get to them, I had to run the gauntlet of the Corots and Millets, etc. etc. which I did very gladly, spending a pleasant hour or so with them. I was especially interested in a little forest picture by Diaz – one of the Barbizon men – being inclined to look on myself as a forest specialist. Standing back, contemplating these little pictures, I seemed to get a clear feeling, though faint and far off, that someday I, too, would be an *artist* and produce similar things. What do you think of that? I then went to the Tate Gallery and had a browse around. I was distinctly cheered and encouraged by my picture seeing." Although there is no written record of it, there is a good chance that MacDonald also saw works by the impressionists, which were being shown regularly by London private dealers by this time.

None of MacDonald's commercial designs of the London period is known to exist, but a few small paintings that survive from the English years reveal a pristine and firm watercolour technique, executed with great care and detail. These still reflect the influence of the Art Students League members, particularly C.M.Manly, but they suggest a growing assurance. In London, MacDonald was seeing quality work in abundance, and his mainly self-taught skills and creative insights were vastly enriched during his four-year stay there.

MacDonald and his family returned to Quebec Avenue late in 1907, and he rejoined Grip Limited as head designer. Before he left the firm in early 1912, three artists with whom his name was to become intimately associated were hired by the firm – Tom Thomson, about 1907, Arthur Lismer and Frank Carmichael, early in 1911. These three added considerably to the sketching activity and painting talk around the studio. Lismer, an Englishman, had studied painting in Sheffield and Antwerp and Carmichael had studied at the Ontario College of Art, but it was to the self-taught Thomson that MacDonald was most drawn. The two men were to become close friends, and until his death in July 1917, Thomson sought out MacDonald as a confidant and adviser. During the years they were to know each other, the two men spent considerable time together. After J.E.H. left Grip, Thomson often used to visit MacDonald's home in Thornhill and, according to MacDonald's son Thoreau, was "considered one of the family, and would drop in whenever the mood moved him for dinner or a chat." Although MacDonald was only four years older than Thomson, he was much more experienced in both design and painting. It has been recorded by their colleagues at Grip that MacDonald encouraged Thomson's budding interest in painting and, with Dr. James MacCallum, persuaded the young bachelor to give up commercial art and become a full-time painter. How much MacDonald influenced Thomson's earlier style in a direct way is open to conjecture. However, there are close stylistic characteristics in their early nocturnes, MacDonald's of 1908 to 1910 and Thomson's of a few years later. Certainly, before he died, Thomson's use of colour and his directness of statement had a balancing impact upon his older colleague. It was MacDonald who designed Thomson's memorial tablet at Canoe Lake.

By 1908, Grip Limited was a beehive of both creative and social activity, with an eminently relaxed atmosphere. Recollections of those who worked there during this period reveal this clearly. MacDonald himself wrote in his unmailed letter to Fred Housser: "There was very little of the 'analytical mind' perceptible around Grip Co. in those days. There was a lot of fun in general and a healthy humility about art, even in the 'bronc' himself, as we used to call Arthur Lismer. ['The damndest bronc you ever saw' is my recollection of the description of Arthur upon his arrival among the bunch.] As for Tom [Thomson], he didn't consciously analyze. He worked from the inside *feeling*, and he let that govern *him*, even sometimes when he produced something that he didn't think he intended."

MacDonald was described in Grip days by a colleague, Leonard Russell: "Mr. Robson [Albert Robson, a biographer of the Group] at that time the Art Director, had a genius for securing the services of any artist of promise, and Grip became noted for the excellent work it turned out. A fine spirit pervaded the Art Room, and through all the fun and the pranks we managed

TO THE MEMORY OF
TOM THOMSON
ARTIST WOODSMAN
AND GUIDE
WHO WAS DROWNED IN CANOE LAKE
JULY 8TH 1917
HE LIVED HUMBLY BUT PASSIONATELY
WITH THE WILD IT MADE HIM BROTHER
TO ALL UNTAMED THINGS OF NATURE
IT DREW HIM APART AND REVEALED
ITSELF WONDERFULLY TO HIM
IT SENT HIM OUT FROM THE WOODS
ONLY TO SHOW THESE REVELATIONS
THROUGH HIS ART AND IT TOOK
HIM TO ITSELF AT LAST
HIS·FELLOW·ARTISTS·AND·OTHER·FRIENDS·AND·ADMIRERS
JOIN·GLADLY·IN·THIS·TRIBUTE·TO
HIS·CHARACTER·AND·GENIUS
HIS·BODY·IS·BURIED·AT
OWEN·SOUND·ONTARIO·NEAR
WHERE·HE·WAS·BORN
AUGUST
1877

Oaks, October Morning, 1909

to turn out a high standard of work. ...At one end of the room sat Jimmy MacDonald, as he was then familiarly known. His desk was covered with sketches, notebooks, paints and brushes, all in utter confusion. It was said that, when he left Grip, he found on his desk material which had been missing for years. ...I do know his table seemed always full and he did his work on one corner. He was a great reader and always had a book on hand to take up in any spare time he had. Although quiet and reserved, he possessed a Scottish sense of humour, was kindly disposed and always willing to help, with keen criticism, any of the younger artists."

It must have been with some feeling of reluctance that MacDonald left Grip in early 1911, although he continued a free-lance arrangement with the firm for several years. It was undoubtedly the contacts and discussions at Grip, and later at the Arts and Letters Club, that led to the eventual forming of the Group of Seven.

It was in 1911 that MacDonald was elected a member of the Arts and Letters Club, a body that had been formed in 1908, and of which Lawren Harris was already a member. Between them, MacDonald and Harris were then the driving forces behind the movement towards a stronger native school of landscape painting. The two men were instantly attracted to one another when they met at the Arts and Letters, and were soon sketching together around Toronto, and later in northern Ontario and Quebec.

The Arts and Letters Club played a vital part in MacDonald's life. Until his death, that vigorous cultural and social institution satisfied much of his need for congenial human contact. Much of his enthusiasm and energy went into club activities, through voluntary contributions of much of his time and talent towards design projects and theatre productions. He was club President from 1928 to 1930. He truly loved the spirit of the club, and it was only fitting, in retrospect, that the Arts and Letters was the site of MacDonald's first one-man show. [He had exhibited with group shows of the Canadian National Exhibition and the Ontario Society of Artists as early as 1908, and was elected a member of the latter society in 1909.]

In November, 1911, nine months after his election to it, the Arts and Letters Club invited MacDonald to show a collection of his recent oil sketches. The result of this was momentous for his career. The brilliance and spontaneity of his little paintings received acclaim from his fellow artist members and he was instantly recognized as one of the foremost painters among them. It was probably Lawren Harris and Dr. James MacCallum [an ardent collector and sponsor of Tom Thomson] who persuaded MacDonald to leave his full time job at Grip to freelance, so that he would have more time to devote to his painting.

C.W.Jefferys, MacDonald's former fellow-member of the Toronto Art Students League and a discerning critic of other people's painting, wrote a noteworthy review of the Arts and Letters Club show in the club's publication, *The Lamps* [December 1911]; "To those of us who are interested in the development of the native spirit in Art in Canada, the quality of this collection and the appreciation of its significance, which the members in general displayed, were equal matters for encouragement."

"For Mr. MacDonald's art is native – as native as the rocks, or the snow, or pine trees, or the lumber drives that are so largely his themes. In themselves, of course, Canadian themes do not make art, Canadian or other; but neither do Canadian themes expressed through European formulas or through European temperaments. In these sketches there is a refreshing absence of Europe, or anything else, save Canada, and J.E.H.MacDonald, and what they have to say; and so deep and compelling has been the native inspiration, that it has, to a very great extent, found through him, a method of expression in paint as native and original as itself. He seems to be able to forget what other men have selected, and how other men have expressed themselves, and in an age of such universal information as ours, and a country so provincial and imitative in its tastes as Canada, these are rare qualities."

Thus, at the Arts and Letters Club in November 1911, MacDonald's career as a painter was seriously launched and his position as a fresh and original talent in Canadian painting recognized.

MacDonald had arrived at his new position as an artist through his spare time labours and experiments. That he achieved so much while supporting his family on his modest salary from Grip is indicative of his industry and devotion to painting. Since he arrived home from England in 1907, he had begun to paint in oils almost exclusively and, for the first time, had ventured into large scale compositions. He exhibited publicly for the first time in the 36th Annual Ontario Society of Artists show of 1908, a canvas entitled *Winter Moonlight*. He was elected to membership in the Society in 1909.

Most of the canvases up to 1911 are clearly marked by his English experience. Unlike many of the small on-the-spot sketches, these larger pieces are, for the most part, darkling, even gloomy, concepts of landscape. Some of them are nocturnes, executed with a tar-like opacity which disturbs the eye and destroys the form. Other canvases have an unpleasant, woolly overall impasto, reflecting the artist's determination to achieve effect with an overdiligent brush and palette knife. There is an attempt to eke out the maximum dramatic effect from low-key atmospheric effects, recalling the artist's early London affection for such Barbizon masters as Narcisse

Chipmunk Point, 1911

Virgil Diaz and Théodore Rousseau. In MacDonald's hands, their romanticism became somewhat strained and a little desperate, yet MacDonald must have learned a great deal from these dogged efforts.

Towards the end of these experiments, however, he painted a number of pictures in which the drama of weather and light emerges in a highly evocative way, and in which the forms and technique are well under control. Such a work is *Wind, Rain and Sunshine, October* [Mr. P.G.McCready Collection] of 1910. MacDonald had clearly learned much from studying the small Constable sketches at the Victoria and Albert Museum. The work also reveals in a masterful fashion, MacDonald's life-long love of cloud effects. The design of the long, curling ribbons of light and the sunlit horizon to the left shows his increasing command of space arrangement, which was to emerge so dramatically within the next few years. He was now integrating his mastery as a graphic designer into his observations as a painter, a marriage which was shortly to lead to such telling compositions as Tracks and Traffic and A Rapid in the North.

Wind, Rain and Sunshine, October, 1910

Morning Shadows, 1912

Morning After Snow, High Park, 1912

Winter Sketch, 1912

Tracks and Traffic, 1912

Thomson's Rapids, Magnetawan River, 1912

Song of the Rapids, 1913

Saw-Mill, Lake Cecebe, 1912

Clouds and Rock, Split Rock, 1912

Sunlit Water, 1912

August Haze, Georgian Bay, 1912

Early Evening, Winter, 1912

Spring Breezes, High Park, 1912

In the Pine Shadows, Moonlight, c 1912

41

Belgium, 1915

The Tangled Garden

By early 1912, released from the day-to-day demands of Grip, MacDonald was free to sketch with his new friend, Lawren Harris. The two of them at first painted around Toronto, and later further afield. It is also likely that the two men were in a group of Arts and Letters members who hired a railway car in 1911, to see an exhibition of the *Société des Peintres et Sculpteurs*, whose president was Auguste Rodin, at the Albright Art Gallery in Buffalo. The exhibition ran from November 16 to December 26, and included works by such minor impressionists as Henri Martin, Henri Le Sidaner and Emile Claus. There were also paintings by Eugène Carrière, Jacques Emile Blanche and Jean François Raffaelli, drawings and sculptures by Rodin, plus nine major canvases by the Paris-based Canadian, James Wilson Morrice.

MacDonald's exposure to the *Société des Peintres et Sculpteurs* show may help to explain a huge leap forward made in his painting between 1911 and early 1912, a leap that encompassed colour, composition and his very handling of paint. Broken colour strokes, in the impressionist manner, are apparent in his painting for the first time in such works as Spring Breezes, High Park [National Gallery of Canada], Early Evening, Winter [Art Gallery of Ontario] and, particulary, Tracks and Traffic [Art Gallery of Ontario]. There is now a new subtlety and authority of touch in the artist's rendering which was not evident a year earlier. The brush drawing is clear and firm and traces the forms crisply.

Spring Breezes, High Park is as light as a Sisley or Pissarro, and would not be unworthy of a minor French Impressionist. Its massed clouds form a perfect foil for the delicate, dark lacing of the silhouetted trees which divide the dappled horizon. However, MacDonald's signal work of 1912 is undoubtedly Tracks and Traffic.

Not a large canvas, *Tracks and Traffic* is one of the most closely wrought of all of MacDonald's paintings; every inch of the canvas space is lovingly worked up. It is a totally *involved* picture, and the artist's fascination for his frozen theme emerges eloquently. Tracks and Traffic was clearly MacDonald's first truly notable creation. It was exhibited publicly three times in 1912, at the Ontario Society of Artists, the Canadian National Exhibition and the Winnipeg Gallery. It was also reproduced in that year's English *Studio* magazine, then a signal honour for any painter.

Unlike Monet, who tackled his similar Gare Saint-Lazare theme some ten times, MacDonald got industrial themes out of his system with this one brilliant effort. [The only related thing in his work was a drawing of a polluted city horizon, inscribed Toronto's Smoke Cloud, executed in 1898.] It can only be regretted that the artist did not lend his obvious ability to render such urban subjects to other major works. Tracks and Traffic was clearly a subject that appealed to Mac-

Sunflower Study, Tangled Garden Sketch, 1915

MacDonald by Arthur Lismer

Donald's strong sense of design, with its counterpoint of colour areas and its repeat patterns laced throughout – its gentle horizontal lines woven together by the repeated verticals of the telephone poles, gas tank and lumber piles. It is hardly, however, a work of grim realism. It is industry transformed into visual poetry, but none the less impressive for that. There are no cinders in this frozen billowing smoke, only a graceful pattern of subtle, mother of pearl tones.

It has been suggested that Claude Monet might have been influenced towards his railway motif by Turner's Rain, Steam and Speed which he had seen in London. It is just possible that MacDonald, in turn, may have seen a reproduction of one of Monet's Gare Saint-Lazare pictures of the 1870s, since there is such a real correspondence between the French master's treatment and the Canadian's vision of the Toronto waterfront railway yards. Certainly, like Monet, MacDonald would have seen Turner's masterpiece in London.

Tracks and Traffic was only one of six canvases MacDonald showed at the Ontario Society of Artists in 1912. The other major work was *Morning Shadows* [Ontario Government Collection], a painting about the same size as Tracks and Traffic and equally concerned with light, but light of a different character. Morning Shadows was one of several 1912 paintings in which MacDonald experimented with cast shadows as the major feature of his compositions. *In the Pine Shadows, Moonlight* [National Gallery of Canada] is a related work of the period. Both paintings feature large foreground areas of shadow tracery thrown by trees which are out of view of the composition area, and the entire basis of the design is placed upon the image cast by the unseen growth. Both of these snow scenes feature figures, a rarity in MacDonald's paintings and limited mostly to the works done around this date. Morning Shadows and In the Pine Shadows, Moonlight were important to MacDonald for a more practical reason; they were the first of his works to be purchased for public collections. Morning Shadows was bought by the Ontario Government for two hundred and fifty dollars, and In the Pine Shadows, Moonlight was acquired from the 1912 Canadian National Exhibition art show by the National Gallery of Canada, his first museum sponsor. The National Gallery was to support MacDonald by an annual purchase for the next five years. Further official recognition was capped in 1912 by his election as an Associate of the Royal Canadian Academy. MacDonald's 1912 paintings also received a warm welcome from the press.

Saturday Night commented on March 16, "Mr. J.E.H.MacDonald is the bright, particular feature of the Fortieth Annual Exhibition of the Ontario Society of Artists. Mr. MacDonald has been known for some time among artists as a painter of beautiful sketches. But now for the first time he has made public demonstration of his ability to paint pictures, and to get into the larger canvases the qualities which distinguish his sketches. Mr. MacDonald seems equally at home in both. His sketches are distinguished by fine design, brilliant colouring, sincerity and a very original point of view. And the pictures possess the same qualities."

Despite such critical success, MacDonald had financial difficulties now that he was without regular employment. Never a strong man, he was pushing himself at both painting and free-lance commercial art. "I have been exceptionally busy all the time," he wrote to his wife during the summer of 1912, "and frequently almost tired out and weary of the job. But of course that feeling comes to all of us, whatever the job. So we will 'begin again and go on'. I am not quite finished at the Fair [the Canadian National Exhibition], but I expect to get through tomorrow evening, in fact, I shall have to call it finished then, as I can hardly afford to put in any more time on it." [MacDonald continued to design and execute CNE displays for the next twenty years. One of his assistants in the early 1920s was A.J.Casson, later a member of the Group of Seven.]

In August of 1912, MacDonald left Toronto for Burks Falls in the Muskoka region of Ontario, about forty miles east of Georgian Bay. From 1909 onward, he and his family went regularly to that northern community to stay with his wife's aunt, Esther A.Prior. Fortunately for the artist, the Burks Falls area offered plenty of material for a landscape painter. The Magnetawan River ran through town on its way to Georgian Bay, and MacDonald did sketches for a number of his works along its banks. Burks Falls was also only a short distance from Go Home Bay, where Dr. James MacCallum owned the island to which the artist had first been invited to paint in 1911. MacDonald and MacCallum became firm friends, and the former would visit the doctor's cottage with his son Thoreau for many years. Over those years, MacCallum acquired a large group of Mac-Donald's works, some as gifts and others by purchase.

Although Georgian Bay is not as closely associated with MacDonald as it is with some other members of the Group of Seven, he painted a number of canvases of the area from MacCallum's island, including *August Haze, Georgian Bay* [Mr. Max Merkur Collection] of 1912 and the large *Fine Weather, Georgian Bay* of 1913 [Private Collection]. Many of MacDonald's earliest Georgian Bay impressions are of sky and water in repose. There is no threat in the metallic blue skies with their puffs of white cloud, and the long, calm horizons which rest beneath them, in contrast to the dramatic Lonely North of 1913 and The Elements of 1916, with their bruise-coloured clouds.

It was near Burks Falls in August 1912, that MacDonald did the small oil studies for two of his finest 1913 paintings, *A Rapid in the North* [Art Gallery of Hamilton] and *The Song of the Rapid*

MacDonald by Frank (Franz) Johnston

View from Split Rock, 1912

[Private Collection], a pair of canvases closely related in theme and identical in size. They are close-up studies, vibrating with crisp, stabbing brush strokes that trace the foaming passage of the rapids. No other Canadian painter, even Maurice Cullen, captured the movement of water in as compelling a manner as did MacDonald. For some years the artist repeatedly tackled the difficult pictorial task of expressing such an elusive theme, and the two Magnetawan River compositions were only the first of those canvases of rushing water which led to such masterpieces as Leaves in the Brook; Falls, Montreal River; The Wild River; and Algoma Waterfall.

By early 1913, MacDonald and Lawren Harris were linked in the minds of their fellow painters as the two leaders or "conspirators" of a new school of Canadian painting. In January 1913, the pair went to Buffalo to view an exhibition of Scandinavian art at the Albright Art Gallery. The timing of their visit was seminal for their ideas and their painting. The subject matter and style of the Scandinavian painters coincided with their own vision of a Canadian landscape style. This was not an unexpected response, since the artists of Sweden and Norway were dealing with a landscape which was essentially like that of Northern Ontario and their style, not unlike that already becoming evident in MacDonald's own development, was essentially based on a rugged brand of impressionism. In a very real way, the art of the Group of Seven and Tom Thomson was a repetition of what had earlier taken place in Sweden, Norway and particularly, Russia.

Hazy Sunshine, Near Split Rock, 1912

Certainly, MacDonald and Harris were excited by what they saw in Buffalo. "Contemporary Scandinavian Art" [January 4 – 26] was a large and important exhibition of 165 works by 45 artists. It was organized by the American-Scandinavian Society under the royal patronage of Sweden, Denmark and Norway, and it travelled to New York, Toledo, Chicago and Boston, as well as Buffalo. It had a strong cultural impact in the United States as well as Canada. For the first time, the New World was seeing some of the artists who were to become major international masters of the twentieth-century. In the show, there were six paintings by Edvard Munch, including such masterpieces as The Sick Child, Summer Night and Starlit Night. There were eight sculptures by Carl Milles, as well as paintings by the then better-known Anders Zorn. But it was the vigorous landscape art by Gustaf Fjaestad, Anna Boberg, Thorlof Holmboe, Otto Hesselbom and Harald Sohlberg that held the attention of MacDonald and Harris at the time.

Nineteen years after the Scandinavian show, in a lecture given at the Art Gallery of Toronto on April 17, 1932, MacDonald still recalled the 1913 exhibition with enthusiasm: "Harris and I were fortunate in this exhibition. We were full of associated ideas. Not that we had ever been to Scandinavia, but we had feelings of height and breadth and depth and colour and sunshine and solemnity and new wonder about our own country, and we were pretty pleased to find a correspondence with these feelings of ours, not only in the general attitude of the Scandinavian artists, but also in the natural aspects of their countries. Except in minor points, the pictures might all have been Canadian, and we felt 'This is what we want to do with Canada.'

"I trust it is no reflection on Canada to say that there was a sort of rustic simplicity about the show which pleased us. It seemed an art of the soil and woods and waters and rock and sky. ...It was not at all Parisian or fashionable. The artists seemed to be a lot of men not trying to *express themselves* so much as trying to express something that took hold of *themselves*. The painters began with nature rather than with *art*. They could be understood and enjoyed without metaphysics, or the frosty condescensions of super critics on *volumes* and *dimensions*, and other art paraphernalia. ...It was this song of praise of their countries that captured our susceptible Canadian souls in Buffalo."

A present day reader of these lecture notes cannot help but think of MacDonald's Magnetawan River paintings and of Thomson's Rapids, painted the same year as the Buffalo trip, when he comes across these comments on the art of Gustaf Fjaestad: "The flow and ripple of water were beautifully painted by him, and shaded streams and stony rapids, and mottled rocks, and spotted birch trunks. We were so fond of these things ourselves that we couldn't but like the pictures, and we were well assured that no Swedish brook or river would speak a language unknown to us and that we would know our own snows and rivers the better for Fjaestad's revelations. ...It seemed to us that the Scandinavians were at least 25 years ahead of us in seizing their opportunities. ...My chief wish has been to make you feel as Harris and I felt that day in Buffalo. 'This is what we want to do with Canada'."

There can be little doubt that the Scandinavian show did affect MacDonald's work, fortifying his own thinking and directly influencing his future painting. Such famous canvases as The Tangled Garden, The Elements, Leaves in the Brook and The Solemn Land would not have taken the form they did if it were not for the artist's exposure to the Buffalo show.

MacDonald's own work received its first foreign exposure in March of 1913, when he exhibited with eight other invited Canadian artists at the MacDowell Club of New York, at 108 West Fifty-Fifth Street [March 6-18]. His co-exhibitors were J.W.Beatty, William Brymner, W.H.Clapp, Maurice Cullen, Clarence Gagnon, E.Wyly Grier, Lawren Harris and C.W.Jefferys. MacDonald showed eight works, including Spring Breezes and A Rapid in the North.

In late spring of 1913 MacDonald and his family moved from 108 Glenlake Avenue to Thornhill, then a village seven miles north of Toronto. [The MacDonalds had left Quebec Avenue for Glenlake when residential developers began chopping down the trees in the area.] Thornhill was a country refuge for artists; Fred Varley, Arthur Lismer, Frank Johnston and Frank Carmichael, all future members of the Group of Seven, came to live there shortly after MacDonald. MacDonald at first rented a small red brick house at 14 Centre Street, and two years later moved across the road to 121 Centre Street, a four-acre lot containing woods of maple, spruce and elms, with a running stream and a ten-room clapboard house. "Four Elms", as MacDonald called the property, also gave him plenty of scope for his favorite hobby of gardening. More importantly, it provided him with subject matter for a number of his finest paintings, including The Tangled Garden. Although, for financial reasons, MacDonald sometimes rented out "Four Elms", he retained ownership of the Thornhill home and his son Thoreau lives there at the time of writing.

As soon as he had settled into 121 Centre Street, MacDonald left on a painting trip with Lawren Harris to Mattawa, on the Ottawa River. They travelled by train via North Bay, and MacDonald wrote with enthusiasm of his first experience with a sleeping car. But he had less praise for North Bay as it was then: "Our train was late at North Bay and we had to put in over an hour waiting for it. We walked about the town a little and found it ugly as an English mining village. Both decided not to move to North Bay. Lawren would prefer New York." Mattawa itself, however, delighted him.

From his first contact with it before 1910, MacDonald felt at one with the north country, its wilderness and small communities, whether Burks Falls, Gull River, Minden or Mattawa. With a typical response, he wrote his wife from Mattawa House: "Here we are out in the open under the soft grey mountain which is the prospect of Quebec. I wish I could send you down some of this fine north country air if nothing else. It certainly feels, especially in the morning, like that air that Henry Thoreau writes about, that morning air which he wanted to bottle and keep on draught against old age." He also wrote of the primeval grandeur that he found around Mattawa, which introduced him to a different topography from that of Burks Falls and Georgian Bay, and was perhaps a small dress rehearsal for Algoma.

MacDonald made his usual trip to Burks Falls in 1913, and then, in late September, joined Lawren Harris on a trip to the Laurentians. They made their headquarters at the Hotel Daoust, in St. Jovite, some sixty miles north west of Montreal. Both MacDonald and Harris responded warmly to the landscape around St. Jovite. "Lawren and I have been doing nothing but admire one fine view after another," MacDonald wrote to his wife, "between sketches and meals. It is certainly a great country this, and I cannot understand anyone going to the Highlands to paint, with Highlands like this in our own country, finer, I should judge, than the older ones by far. I wish you could be down here to see them. I have picked out several fine sites for a cottage, so that when our ship comes in with health and wealth for all of us, we'll know where to come. The

Georgian Bay Island

Laurentian Storm, 1913

colouring is very fine. The trees are well turned, and I have never seen such brilliance of colour or such masses of it. But don't expect our sketches to show it. We have been following lamely after it, hoping to catch up to it some day. ...The weather has been rather trying, very rainy, but picturesque in cloud and atmosphere. We have managed to work steadily, thanks to our umbrellas and the wind shield. When the rain was on, we turned the wind shield into a roof, and we were as comfortable under it as gypsies under a hedge. ...I wish we could live in these Laurentions for a few months. They are full of the most inspiring motifs for an artist and I am sure that in harvest and spring time they would be superb."

Despite MacDonald's delight in the Laurentians, he produced only a few canvases from his sketches done at St. Jovite, and he never did realize his ambition to spend an extended period in the area. Of the Laurentian canvases, the most successful were *Laurentian Hillside, October* [Private Collection] and *Laurentian Village, October* [Hart House, University of Toronto]. Laurentian Hillside, October was the most brilliant colour composition the artist had yet achieved. Fresh and direct in handling, it suggested his future triumphs.

It was in May 1913, that MacDonald first met A.Y. Jackson, at the Arts and Letters Club, although the two men had corresponded since 1910. Jackson had first seen a MacDonald painting in Montreal, at the Royal Canadian Academy exhibition of 1910, a canvas entitled Grey Winter. MacDonald had first seen Jackson's work in Toronto that same year, and had begun writing to the Montreal painter. In a tribute to MacDonald written for the *Canadian Forum* in January 1933, which has a number of inaccuracies, Jackson recalls that MacDonald's letters "were imbued with quiet enthusiasm, some of them full of wisdom and humour and already expressing the idea that, if our art was ever going to be anything, it would have to be homemade and quite unlike the Barbizon and Dutch work which was thought so much of in Canada at that time." Jackson recalled MacDonald painting to be "happy as a child, working out strange rhythms and designs on canvas."

By January 1914, MacDonald and Jackson were neighbours in the newly opened Studio Building constructed by Lawren Harris and Dr. James MacCallum as a "home for Canadian art". Located in a grassy ravine, just north of Bloor and Yonge Streets, the Studio Building at 25 Severn Street eventually became the unofficial headquarters of the Group of Seven. It was designed by architect Eden Smith, with every comfort and amenity an artist could desire. The vast studios, with their fourteen-foot ceilings and large north windows, invited the production of large, major works, and most of the painters took advantage of the opportunity. In the beginning, MacDonald was located in Studio 6 on the top floor, but he moved to the main floor in 1917 after an illness which made it more difficult to climb to the top. About the Studio Building, of which he was a one-time tenant Thoreau MacDonald has written: "The importance of the decision by Harris and Dr. MacCallum to build and finance the Studio Building can't be overestimated. It made a centre and focus for the Group of Seven and their best work might never have been done without it." Certainly MacDonald's most famous canvases were painted in his Severn Street studio.

In March 1914, MacDonald made his first visit to Algonquin Park where he and J.W.Beatty joined A.Y.Jackson, who had already been in the park for a month. In Algonquin, MacDonald did a large number of sketches, but the few canvases done from these cannot, with one exception, be included among his most successful works. In the largest and most important of the Algonquin canvases, *March Evening, Northland* [National Gallery of Canada], one almost suspects the passing influence of J.W.Beatty, although it is an effective atmospheric study in its own right. The smaller Algonquin canvases appear both fudgy in surface and ill-resolved in form. Later in 1914, MacDonald made trips to Minden and to the Gatineau River. He did a series of brilliant on-the-spot studies in both locations, including the superb sketch [Art Gallery of Windsor] for the major 1915 canvas, Logs on the Gatineau [Mendel Art Gallery, Saskatoon].

Two of the most successful paintings of 1914 were both entitled *Edge of Town*. They show a distant view of Toronto, probably from High Park, with small, winter-clad figures in the foreground. These works are closely related in feeling and concept to Morning Shadows of 1912, and are a reminder that MacDonald's progress as an artist was not a straight evolution. From time to time, he would return to an earlier stylistic phase and enlarge upon it. There were years, such as 1914 and 1915, when he seemed to be marking time before moving on in 1916 to a dramatic leap in concept and technique.

Although the 1915 canvases showed no great advance in the artist's approach to painting, *Logs on the Gatineau* is an eminently satisfying work, with some relationship to the 1913 Magnetawan rapid pictures. Its point of view, however, is much broader, and it encompasses a large area of hillside with a typically handled expanse of rushing water beneath it. A less monumental theme, but one of great nostalgic charm, is *Winter Sunshine* [Art Gallery of Hamilton] painted in the winter of 1914-15 from sketches made at Thornhill. It belongs to that group of the artist's works done over a period of years which owe a real debt to impressionism. It is one of the most light-filled and serene of all of MacDonald's landscapes.

In 1916, MacDonald completed a number of canvases that were pivotal for his career and for Canadian art. These paintings, which include The Tangled Garden, The Elements and Autumn

Garden Sketch 3, 1916

Colour [also known as Rock and Maple], rate highly in any list of his major works. They also brought MacDonald a notoriety he never sought when they were exhibited at the 1916 Ontario Society of Artists exhibition.

It would be difficult to imagine three more contrasting portrayals of nature than these canvases present. *The Tangled Garden* is a portrait of a country garden on a hot, lazy summer afternoon. It is suffused with sunshine and cluttered with a lush display of blossoms. It is nature at her most fruitful, parading her visual panoply at its richest. The scene is MacDonald's own Thornhill garden, located just west of his house, and from that simple plot he wrought a Canadian masterpiece.

Though riotous in its impact of growth, The Tangled Garden is bound together in its diverse elements by a very deliberate design. The blossom-heavy sunflowers are arranged so that their stems bend in repeat arabasques across the canvas, weaving the brilliant undergrowth together with their repeated verticals. The open areas of horizontal boards of the horse barn in the background carry a pattern of relief areas across the background to bind the foliage together and emphasize the tranquility of the setting. The colour counterpoint of complementaries – yellows and purples, reds and greens – is as consciously contrived as the rest of the composition. The overall effect, however, is one of intimacy. The seeming abandonment of this close-up of blossoms upset the critics of the period, as did the virtuoso brushwork, which draws the forms so freely, yet with such understanding. There is a total respect for natural texture and delineation of observed shapes. Today, it seems almost unbelievable that such a festive portrait of natural beauty could have been condemned as "an incoherent mass of colour". Yet it is a painting that brought MacDonald a reputation as a revolutionary artist and the leader of a bilious assault upon the public vision.

MacDonald, himself, considered The Tangled Garden one of his major efforts. He prepared for it carefully, with two full composition oil sketches, in the summer of 1915, plus a close-up study of the sunflower and a number of drawings. The sketches for The Tangled Garden are sometimes dated as being done in 1916, although this would have been impossible, since the painting itself was completed before the spring of 1916. There are a number of sketches of sunflowers and other blossoms painted by MacDonald in his garden at the same period, but these are not, as is sometimes claimed, related directly to The Tangled Garden. There are only two complete sketches for it, one, which formerly belonged to Arthur Lismer, in the collection of the National Gallery of Canada, and the other owned by Mr. W.A.Manford. Evidence that MacDonald rated The Tangled Garden highly is the price he put upon it – five hundred dollars – the highest amount he had ever asked until then and only two hundred dollars less than he wanted for another masterpiece, The Solemn Land, five years later.

The Tangled Garden triumphantly joins the designer and painter in MacDonald. Carefully and masterfully designed, it nevertheless retains much of the impetuosity of execution of an on-the-spot sketch. It has been one of the most controversial and beloved of all Canadian paintings. Yet it blossomed in vain, unsold, for several decades until it finally found its permanent, public home by donation to the National Gallery of Canada in 1939.

In contrast to the peaceful fecundity of The Tangled Garden, *The Elements* reveals the dark angry face of nature. It is low in key and lowering in mood. If The Tangled Garden may be called lyric, then The Elements could be fairly described as epic. It is relentlessly challenging in both style and theme. In it, MacDonald reveals the dramatic side of his talent. There is no suggestion of sun-shot impressionism here; instead we find a broad, forceful technique more closely akin to expressionism. The small, huddled figures in the centre of the canvas are almost swallowed up in the vortex of violent brush strokes which delineate clouds, rocks and foliage with an identical bravura. To further emphasize his pictorial effect, the artist has restricted his palette mostly to earth colours and blues.

Although The Elements is a raw, emotional picture, MacDonald had some second thoughts about it some time after it was shown at the 1916 Ontario Society of Artists exhibition, and he repainted parts of it before the 1926 Group of Seven show. The locale of The Elements is Jack-Knife Island in Georgian Bay, and the painting foretold other famous portrayals of the region such as Varley's Stormy Weather, Georgian Bay and Lismer's September Gale of five years later.

For sheer brilliance of hue, *Autumn Colour* [originally titled *Rock and Maple*] is equalled by few of MacDonald's works. Painted with the untramelled directness of a sketch, it is a joyous fragment of the north country along the Moon River near where it flows into Georgian Bay. Commonplace enough in theme, it has been transformed by the audacious play of MacDonald's brush into a radiant creative triumph.

MacDonald's paintings of 1916, to his surprise, were singled out for strong criticism and abuse by the press. The character of his best paintings of that year left most of the reviewers in doubt. They had never encountered such vibrant personal expression before, and as a result, their perplexity was very real.

In the *Toronto Star* of March 11, 1916, "M.L.A.F." writes: "On the whole, the work of the younger

Tangled Garden Sketch, 1915

men dominate the galleries, not so much as to numbers, but as to forcefulness, as to their use of strong, even violent colour. ... Of these, Mr. J.E.H.MacDonald's 'The Tangled Garden' is a good example. It is what one might call 'an incoherent mass of colour', for at first glance, it seems a purposeless medley of crude colours which gradually explain themselves as standing for blooms in a flower bed in full sunshine."

On the same day, the Toronto *Globe* reviewer commented: "There is nothing of the chastened spirit of wartime about the exhibition of the Ontario Society of Artists which was opened in the Reference Library galleries last night. Modern methods are in full flower, Impressionism, Futurism and Cubism flaunt their broad lines and indecipherable flourishes ... The colourists, the moderns, the technicians triumph, and there is no need to go to Scandinavia, or Munich or New York to study the extreme ... Almost from start to finish the exhibition is a blaze of colour. It is the most pronounced departure from realism that has yet been seen here. First position is given to Mr. J.E.H. MacDonald's 'The Tangled Garden', an impressionistic treatment on a massive scale of an old garden with drooping sun flowers and other old fashioned plants in bloom. The same artist shows 'The Elements' which is a grotesque formation of clouds, rocks and water."

These two reviews, while critical, could hardly have been enough to goad the usually reserved MacDonald into a bitter counter-attack. The comments which undoubtedly upset him to the point of anger appeared in *Saturday Night* on March 18, 1916, in a review entitled "Pictures That Can Be Heard" written by Hector Charlesworth: "The chief offender seems to be J.E.H.Mac-Donald who certainly does throw his paint pots in the face of the public. That Mr. MacDonald is a gifted man who can do something worthwhile when he sets his mind to it, is shown in his *Laurentian Village, October* which is well composed and rich and subdued in colour. Across the gallery from it, however, is *The Tangled Garden* which a discriminating spectator attempted to praise by saying it was not half as bad as it looked. In the first place the size of the canvas is much too large for the relative importance of the subject, and the crudity of the colours, rather than delicate tracery of the vegetation seems to have appealed to the painter; but it is a masterpiece as compared with *The Elements* or *Rock and Maple* which for all they convey might just as well have been called *Hungarian Goulash* and *Drunkard's Stomach*." Interestingly enough, Charlesworth did not single out any other artist in the exhibition for such violent criticism. He writes of Lawren Harris admiringly and cites Arthur Lismer and Frank Carmichael with praise.

MacDonald may also have been upset by a second review in the *Toronto Star* which attacked the O.S.A. show in more general terms: "There are some samples of that rough, splashy, meaningless, blatant, plastering and massing of unpleasant colours which seems to be a necessary evil in all Canadian art exhibitions now-a-days."

In any event, MacDonald sat down and wrote a long letter to the Toronto *Globe*, which was published in an edited version on March 27, 1916, under the heading, "Bouquets From A Tangled Garden". [Even in the edited version, the letter was more than a thousand words long.] It is an emotional response, in which MacDonald chooses to answer not only for himself, but on behalf of his associates as well. This letter singled out the mild-mannered, philosophical MacDonald as the ardent leader of the new group of painters in the public mind. It didn't take much in the narrow Canadian art world of 1916 to achieve notoriety.

MacDonald berated the critics: "One would almost think them unaware of the fact that if the function of the artist is to see, the first duty of the critic is to understand what the artist saw. Yet they condemn apparently without understanding and without making any effort to understand. … They affect to 'hear' pictures, to 'smell' them and to 'taste' them, but it must be granted that they do not claim to have seen the pictures they criticize adversely, their sensibilities apparently being too shocked for pretension. … Men to whom a tangled garden is as foreign as an Indian jungle, who are better acquainted with the footlights than sunshine, who may never have seen a bit of rocky Canadian shore in the bright sunshine of an October morning, who were perhaps 'Dancing Around Al Jolson' when the artist was experiencing the dramatic elementalism of Georgian Bay, will gaily bang the painter with their windy bladders and whoop about 'the sincere passion for beauty', 'crudity of colour', 'experimental', 'comfortable' and 'interpretative' pictures."

In his own defence, MacDonald stated: "One makes the claim that 'The Tangled Garden' and other pictures abusively condemned by the critics are genuine works of art merely because of their effect upon them, but they may be assured that they were honestly and sincerely produced. Their makers know when 'vaudeville ideals' are in keeping. If they planned to 'hit' anyone anywhere it was in the heart and understanding. They expect Canadian critics to know the distinctive character of their own country and to approve at least an effort made by the artist to communicate his own knowledge of that character. …One may assure the critics that it can be demonstrated that every one of these pictures is sound in composition. Their colour is good, in some instances superlatively good. Not one of them is too large. Their nationality is unmistakeable. …'Tangled Garden', 'Elements' and a host more, are but items in a big idea, the spirit of our native land. The artists hope to keep on striving to enlarge their own conception of that spirit."

The bitter 1916 press controversy over MacDonald's paintings clearly did not help his ability to sell his works. Although the National Gallery of Canada continued to buy a painting each year for several years, he was able to sell little privately. His purchase of the Four Elms property in Thornhill increased his indebtedness, and there is no doubt he was feeling the double pressures of money and criticism. To help out, he borrowed from his father-in-law, J.R.Lavis, and in 1915 listed debts to him of one thousand, five hundred dollars at four and a half percent. He was also paying interest of three hundred and eighty-two dollars a year on the Thornhill property and had a mortgage on an acre of land on Conduit Street, plus taxes on another lot on MacCauley Avenue. Thus it is not surprising that he had financial difficulties when his total income for 1915 was six-hundred and seventy dollars. This included payments from Grip Limited [seventy-five dollars], the Canadian National Exhibition [one hundred and fifty dollars], the Royal Canadian Academy [one hundred dollars]. MacDonald had also begun part-time teaching, and lists two hundred and fifty dollars from "art school" and twenty-eight dollars for "exam papers".

Altogether, MacDonald listed nine different sources of income for the one year, and with such diverse demands upon his time, it seems almost miraculous he was able to continue his substantial output of painting. During late fall of 1915-16, however, he received a commission from Dr. James MacCallum that combined painting with income. MacCallum had decided to commission a number of his artist friends to design small decorative murals for his cottage at Go-Home Bay. MacDonald, Arthur Lismer and Tom Thomson were chosen. Of the twenty-one designs carried out at the time, ten were by MacDonald, eight by Lismer and three by Thomson. [These are now preserved in the National Gallery of Canada.]

The MacCallum commission must have come to MacDonald as a welcome respite from commercial work. He was paid in installments for the decorations: fifteen dollars on October 1, fifty dollars on December 14, fifty dollars on February 15 and twenty-five dollars on April 15. MacDonald painted his designs over the winter of 1915-16, spending most of his time on the largest panel, *The Supply Boat, Trader.* [There has been some debate as to the identification of the boat, but a pencil study of it in one of MacDonald's sketch books is clearly titled "Trader".] The Supply Boat, Trader measures almost four by eight feet and is a bright, animated panel that reveals the artist's consummate skills as a draftsman and designer. It is an ideal example of MacDonald functioning as an illustrator. It authentically breathes the spirit of the Georgian Bay vacation land in high summer, with its high, blue sky and the busy cottagers gathering their supplies and gossip.

The Supply Boat, Trader is one of the most representational of MacDonald's murals for Mac-Callum. Two others represent the inhabitants of Go-Home Bay past and present, and were shaped

The Supply Boat, Trader, c 1915-16

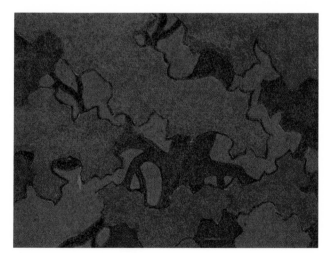

Decorative Panel, Autumn Maple, c 1916

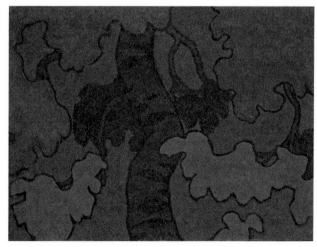

Decorative Panel, Autumn Poplar, c 1916

to flank the cottage fireplace. The panel of the present inhabitants includes a full length portrait of Tom Thomson as a lumberjack. A fourth painting represents A.Y.Jackson sketching against a rocky cliff of his beloved Georgian Bay. Probably the most startling decorations done by MacDonald for MacCallum are six identically sized works. These are unquestionably the most economical and stylized paintings ever carried out by him. They are loosely drawn and richly coloured. They are simplified to the point of near-abstraction and, particularly in the cases of *Autumn Sumach, Autumn Maple* and *Winter Night*, powerful in their pictorial impact. Few other painters of the period would have had the courage to reduce such simple elements to this degree. They are unique in MacDonald's work and make at least one observer wish that the artist had expressed himself more often in such a free, impromptu manner. His innate discipline and long design training would have preserved him from any risk of emptiness.

A Rapid in the North, 1913

Winter Sunshine, 1914

The Shining River Early Spring, 1914

Edge of Town; Winter Sunset, 1914

March Evening, Northland, 1914

The Log Pickers Georgian Bay, 1912

Logs on the Gatineau, 1915

Near Minden, 1916

Autumn Colour (Rock and Maple), 1916

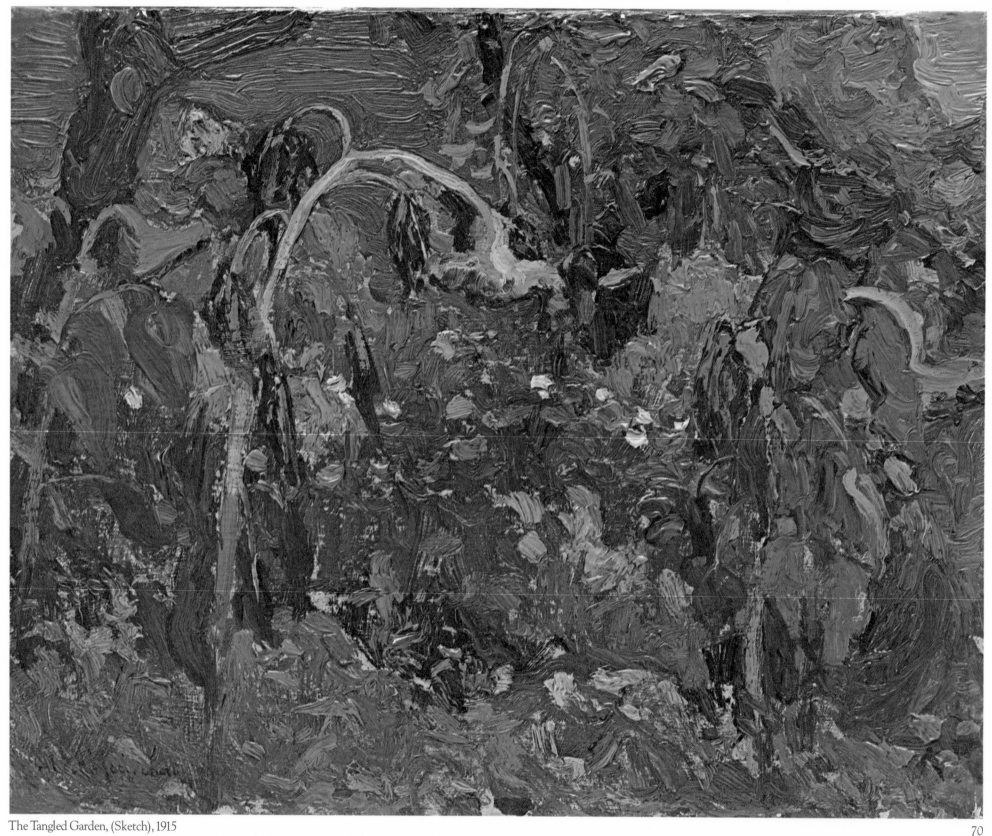

The Tangled Garden, (Sketch), 1915

The Tangled Garden, 1916

The Elements, 1916

Detail–The Elements

Garden Sketch No. 1, (Sunflowers), 1916

Garden Sketch No. 2, 1916

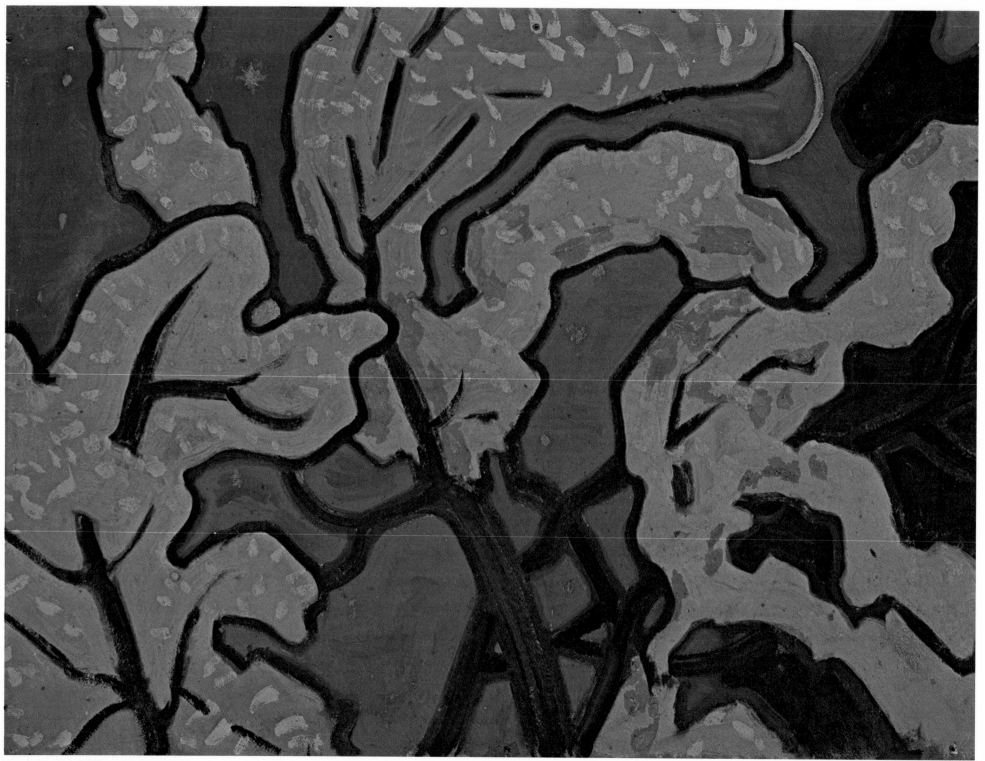

Decorative Panel, Winter Night, c 1916

Decorative Panel, Sumacs, c 1916

Asters and Apples, 1917

Cattle by the Creek, 1918

Nineteen-seventeen was a disastrous year for MacDonald. The growing financial pressures limited his painting, and most of his time was devoted to commercial commissions. The drawn-out war years were disturbing him, like everyone else, and he was depressed by the uncertainty of his wife's health which dated back to the beginning of the century. Despite this, he did manage to complete three canvases, Harvest Evening, Wild Ducks and Asters and Apples.

Harvest Evening is a relatively low-keyed composition which recalls in mood, and even in handling, some of the artist's canvases of five years earlier. Restrained in style and composition, it has a very similar composition to Morning Shadows of 1912. It was one of the last paintings of this twilight character he was to execute. *Wild Ducks* is a singular work. The single figure standing on a rise amidst a multitude of clouds could almost symbolize MacDonald himself. It verges on being a story-telling picture, with its silhouetted subject gazing at the retreating flock of free-flying birds. The mood of the scene certainly reflects, coincidentally or otherwise, the condition of Mac-Donald's life at that time. *Asters and Apples* is the happy, even festive, picture of 1917. It glows with the light of contentment, and reflects MacDonald's own love of gardening. It was painted at Thornhill of the same flower bed that sat for The Tangled Garden. The surety of its brush-work and the clarity of its colour give it a vigour which saves it from sentimentality. The canvas possesses the same celebration of rural life that characterized so much of MacDonald's verse.

In July 1917 Tom Thomson drowned in Canoe Lake, Algonquin Park, at the age of thirty-nine. MacDonald was distraught by the tragedy. He had known Thomson for nine years, and a close association had grown between the two men. MacDonald's artist son, Thoreau, has stated that Thomson had a great respect for his slightly older colleague and often visited MacDonald at his home in Thornhill. MacDonald also had a very real impact upon Thomson's career as an artist, especially in their Grip Limited days.

In his mourning for Thomson, MacDonald wrote an epitaph for his friend, which eventually found its way onto a memorial cairn at Canoe Lake. It read: "To the memory of Tom Thomson, Artist, Woodsman and Guide who was drowned in Canoe Lake July 8th, 1917. He lived humbly but passionately with the wild. It made him brother to all untamed things of nature. It drew him apart and revealed itself wonderfully to him. It sent him out from the woods only to show these revelations through his art. And it took him to itself at last." MacDonald designed the brass plaque upon which the tribute was engraved, but the cairn itself was mainly the work of artist, J.W.Beatty, and a group of friends.

The best record of the building of the memorial is in a letter written by MacDonald to Tom

A.Y.Jackson Sketching, c 1915-16

Thomson's father on October 3, 1917: "I have just returned from Canoe Lake, where I spent the week-end helping Mr. Beatty to put on the plate and give the cairn a few finishing touches. The cairn is a fine piece of work, and with the brass plate in position, it looks quite imposing. It is situated near an old favorite camping spot of Tom's. ... The devotion of practically everyone at Canoe Lake in offering their help has been fine. Mr. J.W. Beatty planned the cairn and directed and did most of the work in connection with its erection. I myself was not able to get to Canoe Lake until the cairn was practically completed, but I had no difficulty appreciating the efforts of those concerned. Most of the stone had to be carried up a steep cliff about sixty feet high. All the sand had to be brought a mile or so by boat and then carried up to the site. There are probably over six tons of material in the cairn." In his letter, MacDonald also apologized to Thomson's father for inscribing Tom's birthplace as "near Owen Sound" when, in fact, it was Claremont, Ontario. It has been suggested that MacDonald had a physical collapse while working on the cairn, but this is pure romantic invention.

In late November 1917, at his wife's urging, MacDonald rented his Thornhill property, and moved to a house some miles south near Pratt's Mill on an eastern branch of the Don River in Hogg's Hollow. They rented the house from Mrs. Oscar Lucille Taylor who, like Joan MacDonald, was a keen Christian Scientist. MacDonald made the move with reluctance, but his wife wanted to be closer to her church. [It was not a question of saving money.] On the day of the move, MacDonald's already frail and overtaxed constitution gave in, and he had a complete physical collapse that left him bedridden for five months. According to his son, Thoreau, the artist's physician, Dr. A.D. Watson, described the illness as a stroke.

During his long illness, MacDonald began to write poetry, renewing an interest that occupied him earlier in a spasmodic way. Now he wrote regularly, at the suggestion of his friend, Barker Fairley, a distinguished scholar and art enthusiast. Though he wrote basically as occupational therapy, much of MacDonald's verse is accomplished and evocative in a direct, lean style. He had read poetry eagerly since boyhood, and his two favourite poets had remained Robert Burns and Walt Whitman. While earlier poems, such as "The Victor", dedicated to explorer Captain Scott, are somewhat fulsome and Kiplingesque in manner, MacDonald's verse dating from his illness is much less affected. Much of it appeared in 1918 and later in *The Rebel* and the *Canadian Forum*. Although a collection of his poetry, entitled *West by East*, was posthumously published in 1933, it has been long out of print, and a few excerpts from his verse deserve to be published here:

The shadows of the orchards trees have made
Their soft diurnal round across the snow;
Netting with blue the rippled drifts below:
Now fused in rosy glow they slowly fade
Over the eastern hill where night arrayed
In deepening blue, brings the glad moon to go
Forth-faring with her, till the morning grow
Through many a skiey field and starry glade.
Heaven laid on earth, O Winter, is thy gain,
Sunshine and snow, – clear beauty without mar;
May the day's blessing still my inward war,
With calming night leading the troubled brain
To follow on to sleep some gentle star,
Shy-peering through the frost-leaves of the pane.
[Winter Evening]

The dark earth lifting through the sinking snow
A high sun riding on the bounding wind.

Far uplands pale against a snow-grey sky
Snow-fence leaning thrown by winter's wind.

The apple prunings in the shrunken drift
Now show new-peeled and shining in the wind.

A girl in rubber boots pumping a pail
Of brimming water whipping in the wind.

Verandah rockers waiting summer time
Bumping and shaken by the restless wind.

The tossing lilac buds against the house
Grip tight their purple secrets from the wind.

And all the orchard trees are looking south
Beyond the beating of the ancient wind.
[March Wind]

The city lifts her glimmering lamps
To shaken tumults of the stars,
And snow-shod on the lonely streets
No traffic jars.

The city trembles as it clings
In a blue valley of the stars;
Snow-hushed the earth, and vast in heaven
Dim, silent wars.
[Winter Night]

The dark barn broods, lofty and wide
Over the crops within, and by its side
The banded silo leans and cattle shove
To feed beneath the straw-stack's hollowed cove.

Shaggy as bears the fur-clad farmers lurch
Along the car stopping beside a church,
A father carries a white bundled child;
The gravestones lean like trees before the wild
Wind nipping the church smoke at the chimney edge
And flinging it by wall and window ledge.
[West by East]

83

During his illness, MacDonald also wrote a number of essays, including "A Hash of Art", a light-hearted satire of students' art history examination papers that MacDonald had marked [*The Rebel*, December 1917]. A second article, "A Whack at Dutch Art" [*The Rebel*, March 1918], is more serious, even bitter, in tone. It introduces an imaginary, wealthy collector of Dutch art named Brown: "If one jokingly asks him where his Canadian pictures are, he offers another cigar, 'No atmosphere in Canada – light too crude'. His idea of atmosphere is something muggy, something that can be handled like a London fog, air that wraps a landscape like wool; a vibrant blue sky and the sparkling Georgian Bay beneath would be too crude and clear for him in pictures, although he actually enjoys such things in his fine yacht, the Flim-Flam. A bright rendering of maple or birch in autumn, or the sun shining on a snow bank would simply dazzle him after his grey Dutch canals, or sheep on a sand dune. After his strenuous day at the office, he does not want to be stimulated. He wants to be put to sleep, and his Dutch art does that for him. Were there any of our connoisseurs who put their faith in Manet, Sisley, Monet, Pissarro, Whistler, Segantini, Cezanne or Gauguin, among others?

"It is not suggested that Canada should be a private preserve for Canadian artists or that they should fall heirs to all that is now expended on foreign art, but one must deplore the fact that many paintings of fine quality, with such modest prices as twenty dollars or thirty dollars remain unsold in our exhibitions, while six hundred dollars or seven hundred dollars is paid for foreign works which would be rejected by the juries of most of our exhibitions." MacDonald then adds what is clearly a note from personal experience: "Many Canadian artists are handicapped by having to devote the greater part of their time to work apart from art, and men of great talent have been discouraged by the indifferent prospects of artists, and the slight esteem in which artists are held.

"The Canadian artist and the lover of Canadian art have been humble long enough. To be so any longer is to degrade a desirable virtue. To reverence great masters and older schools of painting is quite another matter from coming to salute every time a dealer exhibits a picture with a Dutch name on it."

It is clear from his "A Whack at Dutch Art" that while MacDonald's body was weak, his spirit was as resilient as ever.

After April 1918, MacDonald slowly recovered his energies and began to paint again. He managed three canvases during the year, including *Cattle By the Creek* [National Gallery of Canada] and *A Sandy Beach, Lake Ontario* [Mr. Max Merkur]. Cattle By the Creek, painted at Moon

River, is one of the most rigid of all MacDonald's compositions. He was always, of course, a careful designer, but here a self-conscious contrivance shows through. It is a set piece without spontaneity, except for its remarkable colour. Its planes are placed one behind another with an almost cut-out character; water, trees, cows and distance follow flatly behind one another. What MacDonald surely meant as a design to stress the quietness of the summer afternoon, with its unmoving water and perfectly balanced trees, emerges as a stilted arrangement, relieved only by its rich brush strokes and glowing hues. In A Sandy Beach the artist reverts to almost pure impressionism. It is a bright, directly painted, small atmospheric study of sparkling light, and is as close to the pure impressionist manner of Monet as MacDonald was ever to come. In a sense these few pictures of 1918 were only recuperating exercises for the masterpieces which were shortly to follow.

By late August, MacDonald was well enough to be invited by Lawren Harris on a sketching trip to the Algoma region of Northern Ontario. MacDonald at first rejected the idea, insisting that, because of his recent illness, he would hold the other artists back. But Harris persuaded him to agree, a decision that was to prove momentous for Canadian art. For MacDonald, it proved the perfect tonic for his mind and health.

On September 10, Harris, MacDonald, Frank Johnston, Dr. MacCallum and Harris' dog "Prince" left Toronto for Algoma. It was to be the first of the two now famous "box-car" trips. They made three stops on the journey, first near Agawa Station, a second at Hubert and the third at Batchewana, and MacDonald reported home from all of them. The CPR box-car in which the three artists and Dr. MacCallum lived for almost a month was fitted with bunks, a stove, a water tank and sink, a kitchen bench and shelves, bracket lamps and a couple of lanterns, and a large cupboard for supplies. The four men lived, in other words, in something of the relative comfort of a simple modern camping van. They had plenty of food and books. On that 1918 trip, Mac-Donald usually stayed close to the box-car home, so that he could rest when necessary, although he made a few trips along the tracks by hand-car. Most of his triumphant sketches of that year were done from the tracks of the Algoma Central Railway, looking over the great autumn panoramas, or down into the great canyons with their rushing rivers and waterfalls.

From his arrival, MacDonald was ecstatic about the Algoma landscape. It suited perfectly his romantic nature and the pantheist in him. The sculptured hills and their forests exalted him, and he put them down as he found them. As A.Y. Jackson wrote after MacDonald's death, "What Thomson was to the Algonquin country, MacDonald was to Algoma" [*Canadian Forum*, January 1933].

northern Pine.   J.E.H. MacDonald '15

Layton's Lake, Algoma, 1919

"I will not attempt to describe this country for you," MacDonald wrote, shortly after his arrival at Agawa, "as I haven't a great flow of language at present. Perhaps that will come as usual when I get back and talk as usual after a trip. But the country is certainly all that Lawren and the Dr. said about it. It is a land after Dante's heart. The canyon is like a winding way to the lower regions and last night, when the train went through just after dark, with the fireman stoking up, the light of the fire shining on the smoke clouds, it was easy to imagine his Satanic majesty taking a drive through his domain. I had walked a little distance up the canyon and the effect was eerie enough to make me speed up for home. The great perpendicular rocks seemed to overhang as though they might fall any minute, and the dark Agawa moving quietly through it all had an uncanny snakiness. On a fine day, such as this, the canyon seems to lead *upwards*, and has all the attributes of an imagined Paradise, excepting, perhaps, anything in the way of meadows. There are beautiful waterfalls on all sides, and the finest trees – spruce, elm and pine. It is a Shelly-like kind of place and certainly would make a great background for gods and goddesses, either white or red.

"I think the most impressive sight I have had on this trip was a view of Lake Superior from a place about eight miles from here on the way up. The railway is there within about four miles of the lake, probably 1500 feet above it, commanding a wonderful view of craggy hills, waterfalls and the winding Agawa. I have never seen anything so impressive as the half-revealed extensiveness of the lake. There was a sharpness in the air which merged the horizon with the sky and that smooth shimmering infinity of waters was like a glimpse of God himself. I have not assimilated this experience yet. It is something to be quiet about and think over. It reminds one of Paul, being caught up and hearing unutterable things. ..."Am glad to say I am feeling much better. All of us are working full time, especially Lawren and F."

After he had been at Agawa Station for a week, his enthusiasm was unabated. "This seems to be the original site of the Garden of Eden," he wrote home on September 18. "It is most like fairy-land or goblinland of any I have seen. My trip yesterday with the old man [a section hand] took me to the entrance of the canyon and the great rocks tower up everywhere like old German fairy castles. The place is remarkably quiet. ...The leaves are turning very slowly. ...Leaving for Hubert in the morning."

Even in his painter's paradise of Algoma, however, MacDonald was still pursued by concerns back home. "I am rather concerned about the problem," he wrote his wife. "It seems as though such things had no existence here, but I suppose they must be faced some day. I hope to get back in good condition to help in their resolution, and in the meantime will do what I can in having the right attitude towards them. I hope you will not be too worried about things."

MacDonald was now forty-five years of age, and on the verge of his greatest work. He made two more trips to Algoma. On September 17, 1919, he returned on the second "box-car" trip with Harris and Johnston. This time they were joined by A.Y.Jackson. The journey repeated the same three stops as 1918. It was about this 1919 trip that MacDonald wrote his article, "A.C.R.10557" in the Arts and Letters magazine, *The Lamps*, in December 1919. [This article has usually been incorrectly described as referring to the first, 1918, Algoma trip.] The box-car on the 1919 journey was a festive affair, complete with a small "Christmas Tree" and a moose skull "topped with sprays of ever-green and red berries" with a design painted beneath it incorporating the motto "Ars Longa, Vita Brevis" and the interwoven initials of the artists. The sketching material aboard included the inevitable umbrellas, used for reducing the sun's glare as much as for rain. MacDonald arrived back in Algoma full of expectations. He wrote his wife from the first stop on September 19, 1919, "Glad to find the old impression of the country pleasantly renewed."

MacDonald, in fact, waxed as eloquent about the Algoma landscape in 1919 as he did in 1918. In "A.C.R.10557" he wrote, "Every day advanced the passing of the leaf, and soon our painters had to go in quest of the desireable 'spot of red'. The hills that had been crimson and scarlet with maple were changed to purplish grey. The yellow leaves were falling fast. They realized one night of breaking cloud that there was a growing moon, and they looked at old star friends from the car door – The Dipper lying flat among the spruce tops, and one rare night bright Capella dimmed in a jet of Aurora. After such a night the trees could resist no longer, and they saw many a one cast off her leaves in one desperate shower. Birch woods, that were dense yellow in the morning, were open grey by night. But the wild cherry leaves still hung as though the high fifes and violins were to finish the concert of colour. They were another of the notable little graces of the bush, daintily hung in every shade from the palest yellow to deep crimson against the big blue-gold hills of the Montreal Valley. ... Two of the rare days of the trip were spent by the workers at the great Falls of the Montreal River, and they had many a good hour on smaller streams. ... It was not long before the painters were packing for their return journey. ... The red canoe was carried up again from the river, the 'pede' [railway hand-car] was taken apart and put aboard, and the crew of A.C.R.10557, swinging round the curves in the rear coach of the mixed train could see that red goddess of theirs, swaying along in her honeymoon decorations, as she clung to a fussy and determined engine headed once more for the Fall of St. Marie." In the fall of 1920 the artists' more mundane headquarters in Algoma was a cottage at Mongoose Lake.

In Algoma, MacDonald found his spiritual home as a painter. In a period of four years, he created from it most of the paintings upon which his reputation for greatness depend. From that region's rolling hills, rushing rivers and hardwood forests, he wrought some of the most memorable canvases in his country's art. Some, like The Solemn Land, became genuine cultural icons.

In MacDonald's small, on-the-spot oil sketches created during his three trips, we already find the astonishing impact Algoma had upon him as an artist. Precisely observed and brilliantly drawn with a free, loaded brush, these little panels reveal a new creative confidence and technical assurance. They are usually designed with all the completeness of a large composition, yet they possess the autographic freshness which belongs to an instant sketch. MacDonald seems to have been on top of his Algoma material from the beginning. His sketches represent a perfect meeting between artist and theme. Looking at them, the viewer can easily imagine MacDonald as his son, Thoreau, often observed him, "In the open he was a fast, expert worker, and it was a pleasure to watch him at it. He swiftly drew in his layout or design, usually with permanent blue, then with nervous energy put down the complete drawing and beautiful unexpected colours of a beaver pond, a tangled swamp or rock slide, all the while with keen and comprehensive looks from landscape to panel. This he thought the finest pleasure in life." Though small in size, usually 8½ X 10½ inches, these little painted pieces of board or wood panel are among the most vivid portrayals of the Canadian earth. MacDonald painted mostly on millboard panels, a bookbinder's board from Brown Brothers in Toronto. His son prepared these for him with a coat of shellac.

During 1919, MacDonald painted his first four Algoma canvases – The Wild River, The Little Falls, Leaves In the Brook and The Beaver Dam. Even in these more considered, larger canvases based on his sketches there is eloquent evidence that the artist's style had undergone a triumphant, seemingly instant change since he visited Algoma. Nowhere in his past work, even in Autumn Colour or The Tangled Garden, is found the audacious, rhythmic handling of pigment we find in *The Wild River* or *Leaves in the Brook*. While the former, his first Algoma canvas, is a slightly disordered design, its forms and textures tossed about with an enthusiastic abandon, it sets the tempo for many of the Algoma works that were to follow.

Where The Wild River is an experimental pictorial shout of release, *Leaves in the Brook* is a more ordered design, without any loss in its compelling energy of statement. It is one of the most spontaneous of all of MacDonald's paintings. The brush calligraphy in it moves without hesitation from one corner of the canvas to another. Nowhere is there a moment of hesitation in the vigorous strokes that draw the forms; foliage, rocks and water are moulded together in what may be fairly described as a joyous impasto. Here is a modest, fleeting vignette of nature made permanent through the compelling mastery of MacDonald's talent. Though small in area, this piece of Canadian woodland looms large as a work of consummate draftsmanship and colour. However, Hector Charlesworth, MacDonald's unremitting critic, wrote in *Saturday Night* on December

13, 1919, that "the overemphasis is thunderous, especially in such a picture as Mr. MacDonald's 'Leaves in the Brook.'"

The Little Falls is a much more static picture, designed in flatter design areas. It is more hesitant in its brush rendering, and its forms, particularly the rocks in the middle ground, lack the bravura assurance of drawing found in Leaves in the Brook. This picture, which was shown in the exhibition, "Algoma Sketches and Pictures by J.E.H.MacDonald, Lawren Harris and Frank H.Johnston" at the Art Gallery of Toronto in 1919, almost certainly preceded Leaves in the Brook, and the latter picture benefitted from the experience MacDonald derived in doing the earlier work. The Little Falls was also an important rehearsal for the triumphant 1920 Algoma Waterfall.

For several years Algoma transformed MacDonald's life, and in paintings such as *Falls, Montreal River* [1920], he pays back in paint the joys that monumental northern land had given him. In this canvas, the high visual drama of the wilderness is transformed into a masterpiece of landscape. In it, MacDonald has brought together all his hard-won skills as designer, draftsman and painter in a personal and epic way. This is certainly one of his most brilliantly orchestrated canvases. Every inch of it is lovingly searched out for the maximum richness of texture and colour. Falls, Montreal River is one of MacDonald's largest works, surpassed in size only by The Wild River and equalled by The Solemn Land, Autumn in Algoma, Forest Wilderness and Rain in the Mountains.

The Solemn Land [1921] is probably MacDonald's best-known Algoma canvas, and one of the most popular of all Canadian landscapes. MacDonald ranked it as one of his finest achievements. When it was first shown, at the Ontario Society of Artists exhibition in 1921, he priced it at seven hundred dollars, his highest figure until that time. The Solemn Land depicts one of those elevated views the artist obtained from the tracks of the Algoma Central Railway. It is truly, as he described it, a panorama for the gods, and he presents it with all the pictorial nobility it deserves. There is a creative hush and a sense of primeval mystery about this picture which in part explains the magic it has held for so many who have come to know it. The only movement to disturb its stillness is the cloud shadow moving across the massive, sun-lit hill in the background. Here, indeed, is the quiet splendour of the unpeopled northland.

Rowanberries [1922] is one of the most festive of all MacDonald's paintings. The ringing vermilion clusters of berries and their branches form an open-work screen through which a sparkling, rock-bordered stream may be seen. Painted with extreme directness in crisply delineating strokes, its palette and execution relate closely to post-impressionism. In the painting of the foreground of the stream it is even reminiscent of Van Gogh. Rowanberries also once more expresses MacDonald's skill as a designer and his affection for decorative plant forms.

Mist Fantasy [1922] stands apart from the rest of the Algoma paintings. With it, MacDonald has transformed Algoma into a Japanese screen, with art-nouveau overtones. Whereas most of his Algoma canvases reflect the vitality of nature, here nature is put carefully in her place, with all of her elements neatly arranged. Here, MacDonald the designer takes clear precedence over the painter. These blue pine trees, red boats, ribbons of mist and the flattened ochre and crimson foliage would have pleased Whistler. The two scarlet boats are almost centred; the outlines are carefully drawn to isolate each shape from the next; the reflections on the water are perfectly passive – all is joined to create a highly stylized composition. There is an air of unreality about this mannered, even elegant, landscape apparition. With Mist Fantasy, MacDonald showed his usual aptness for titles.

Throughout his Algoma period, MacDonald proved again and again that he was a master of the big panorama. It is easy for grand overviews in landscape painting to become monotonous and tiresome, as is proven by countless portrayals of mist-ridden highlands. MacDonald escaped monotony by changing not only the immediate locale, but the technique, mood and compositional treatments of his panoramas. Algoma Wilderness [1921], Autumn in Algoma [1921] and Northland Hilltop [1922-31] present three very different approaches to the subject.

In *Algoma Wilderness* the panorama is directly attacked in a stark manner, with only the hint of a rocky foreground. Its continually receding hills present an uncompromising theme for a painter; but MacDonald has turned an apparently unrewarding view into a radiant masterpiece through his subtly patterned areas of light and shade, and the closely related colour harmonies which range from the blazing scarlet sumach bush in the foreground through mutations of golden ochre and russet to the muted grey-green distance. This carefully wrought composition moves inward through its atmospheric perspective, but it also is kept flat in design by the overall richness of the pigment itself and the subtly-woven brushwork which delineates the retreating forest. He keeps the eye involved in the tenuous conflict he has established between the vast distances of his theme and the countering flat pictorial concept.

In *Autumn in Algoma* the background panorama of hills is vignetted by the rich ornamentation of foreground growth. A wide, clear blue river is mounted within a setting of flaming foliage and remote blue and green hills. The busy brush technique used here is strikingly different from that used in Forest Wilderness and The Solemn Land of the same year. Autumn in Algoma

Hepaticas

Coboconk Village

is accented with short, brisk brush strokes. In colour and handling it is one of the busiest of his paintings, virtually alive with movement. For MacDonald, unlike so many painters, there was never an easy, patented formula.

Northland Hilltop may be referred to as the last Algoma canvas since, although it was painted in 1922, MacDonald repainted it in 1931, the year before his death. As in Autumn in Algoma, the receding panorama is pierced by foreground growth, but in this case by fallen or dying trees.

Northland Hilltop has much of the reserve of texture and colour that marked the mountain pictures the artist was engaged on when he repainted it. It is a bridge picture between styles, but it still must be ranked high among MacDonald's works. The surety of its design and the serenity of its mood make it a fitting farewell painting to the Algoma years.

When the famed Group of Seven held its first exhibition at the Art Gallery of Toronto from May 7 to May 27, 1920, MacDonald included three of his Algoma paintings, The Wild River, The Little Falls and The Beaver Dam. Three of his fellow Group of Seven members, A.Y.Jackson, Lawren Harris and Frank Johnston also showed Algoma canvases. None of the remaining three, F.H.Varley, Franklin Carmichael and Arthur Lismer had yet visited that region. MacDonald continued to feature his Algoma works in most of the succeeding Group of Seven shows. They formed the heart of his representation in Group exhibitions and his fame rested mainly upon them. He showed with the Group in all of its eight exhibitions, until its disbanding in 1931.

As the oldest and most widely published of the men who formed the Group of Seven, MacDonald had led their battle for recognition for almost a decade. While Jackson, Varley and Lismer were active overseas or at home as war artists, he was busy writing articles in their defence and keeping their reputations before the public. With Harris' practical and philosophical support, it was MacDonald's unwavering confidence and conviction in a native Canadian art that most helped to bring about that united determination which led to the formation of the Group of Seven. It may be fairly claimed that MacDonald and Harris were the moving spirits behind the Group of Seven.

In his long article, "The Canadian Spirit in Art" written for the March 4, 1919, *Spectator* [a Canadian magazine, not the English *New Statesman* as incorrectly cited by F.B.Housser in "A Canadian Art Movement" and others], MacDonald sounded a prophetic note for the Group of Seven which was to come into being within less than a year. "The Canadian spirit in art is just entering on possession of its heritage. It is opening a new world, and the soul of the artist responds with the feeling that it is very good. ...It may be claimed that our art movement is now steady and conscious of its aims."

A Sandy Beach, Lake Ontario, 1918

Algoma Woodland, 1918

Young Maples, Algoma, 1918

The Little Falls, (Sketch), 1918

The Little Falls, 1919

Beaver Dam, Algoma, Near Mongoose Lake, 1918

Near Montreal, Lake Algoma, 1919

Gleams on the Hills, (Sketch), 1918

Algoma, Hill, 1919

Near Hubert, Algoma, 1919

Algoma, 1919

Algoma Bush, September, 1919

Lake in the Valley, 1919

Beaver Pond, Algoma, c 1919

Montreal Lake Algoma, c 1919

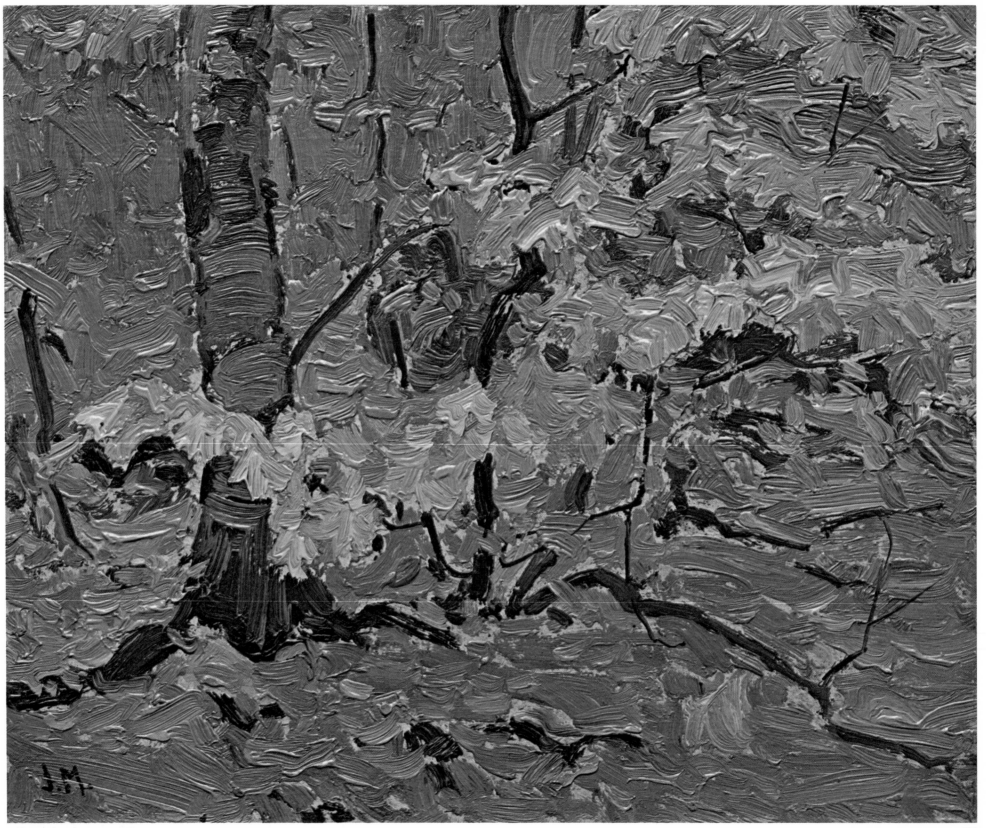

Fall Woods, Algoma, c 1919

Algoma Bush, Autumn, c 1919

Beaver Dam and Birches, 1919

The Beaver Dam, 1919

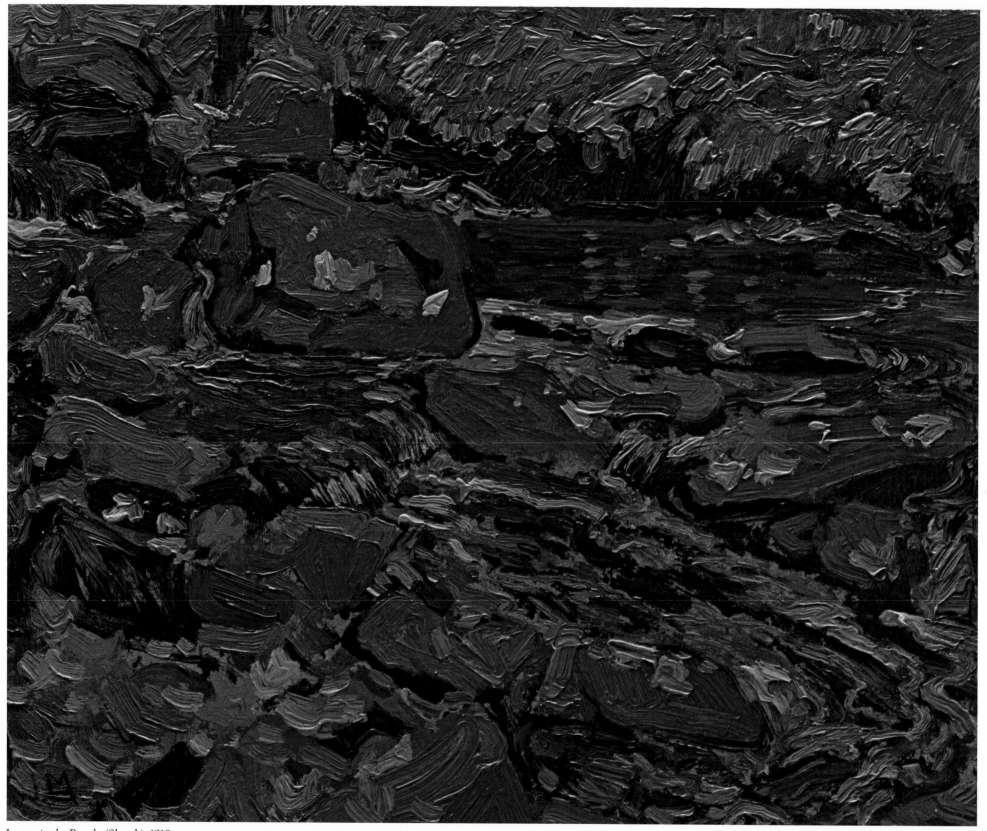

Leaves in the Brook, (Sketch), 1918

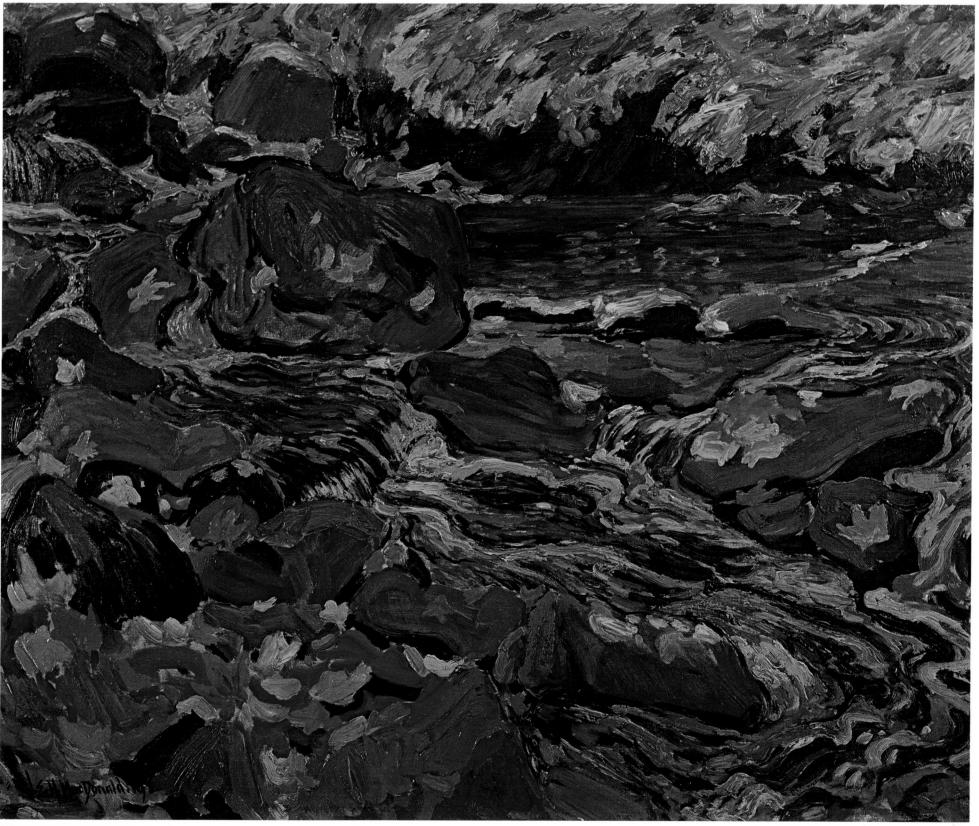

Leaves in the Brook, 1919

Moose Lake, Algoma, 1919

Agawa, 1920

Algoma Hills, 1920

Algoma, c 1920

Sungleams, Algoma Hilltop, 1920

Silver Swamp, Algoma, 1919

Solemn Land, (Sketch), c 1918-19

The Solemn Land, 1921

The Wild River, 1919

Batchawana Rapid, 1920

Algoma Forest, 1920

Autumn in Algoma, 1921

Agawa Valley, c 1920

Autumn Colour, 1920

Autumn Algoma, 1918

Forest Wilderness, 1921

Falls, Montreal River, 1920

Algoma Hilltop, c 1921-22

Mist Fantasy, Sand River, (Sketch), Algoma, c 1919

Mist Fantasy, 1922

Rowanberries, Algoma, 1922

Northland Hilltop, 1931

The Mountains

The 1920 Algoma trip climaxed ten years of virtual freedom from a regular job for MacDonald. He had enjoyed almost a decade of painting and freelance designing, but the monetary rewards had been meagre, and in 1921 he was obliged by financial pressures to accept a full-time teaching post at the Ontario College of Art. This necessary sacrifice of his own painting was a deep loss for Canadian art, but a bonus to a generation of students. MacDonald was a diligent and expert teacher who had more than thirty years of experience in fine and commercial art to share.

Cathedral Mountain, 1925

To be nearer the downtown location of the Ontario College of Art, MacDonald rented a house at 40 Duggan Avenue near the heart of the city while maintaining his Thornhill property and Severn Street studio. For the previous two years, he and his family had been living in the downtown Studio Building.

Artist Carl Schaefer, who was one of MacDonald's first students, recalls him as a "true revolutionary for that period. He was an inspired teacher. He didn't insist on what we must do, but encouraged us to develop our own special talents. He pointed the way, and we did the creative thinking and work." The slim, red-headed MacDonald who taught design and lettering became an instant favourite of the thirty-odd students he taught during his first year. He encouraged them to explore new movements as much as the achievements of the past. His basic advice, recalls Schaefer was, "Think big. Be generous. Don't fiddle. Enlarge yourselves." He was fond of quoting William Blake, "See not *with* but *through* the eye." "Art is an ordering of the material in harmony with the spirit." "Art," MacDonald wrote in his teaching notes, "is the successful communication of a valuable experience."

"MacDonald's blue-grey eyes were always full of humour," says Schaefer. "His comments ranged not only over art but also included literature. He would read from texts to fire our imagination. He was strong on heraldry and the craft school of William Morris, and he introduced his students to figures as diverse as J.M.W. Turner, Walt Whitman, Cezanne, William Blake and Ernest Thompson Seton. He also introduced us to the *avante garde* of the time; the Bloomsbury Group, members like Virginia Woolf, Roger Fry and Clive Bell. Behind all this he gave us the necessary basics of lettering and graphic design." Carl Schaefer, who studied under MacDonald from 1921 to 1924, later became an assistant and friend.

MacDonald was to remain at the Ontario College of Art until his death in 1932. He put a large part of his limited energies into his teaching role, and it seems to have left him continually tired. He also pushed himself with a full schedule of activities. "Everything is surging along,

Artist's Home and Orchard, 1927

smoother or rougher as the track may be," he wrote his wife, who was away visiting the Christian Science Headquarters in Boston in 1928. "I have been to Thornhill this afternoon. A beautiful sunny October afternoon among the sunflowers. Have been very busy all week. Arts and

Letters meeting. Students election at O.C.A. [Ontario College of Art]. School children's exam yesterday at Phoebe Public School. [What it is to be Prime Minister.]"

MacDonald's abilities as teacher and administrator were such that in 1929 he succeeded his old teacher, George A. Reid, as principal of the Art College, after serving as acting principal for a year. Heading an art college is a difficult and demanding position at the best of times. There is a more intense involvement on the part of staff and students than in most educational institutions, and the principal is the obvious target for all parties. In MacDonald's case, the student body threatened to go on strike if he were not chosen to succeed George Reid as head of the college. MacDonald never revealed what his own wishes in that direction may have been, but there is no doubt he would rather have been painting.

In the Sugar Bush

MacDonald put his best efforts into teaching, but he did not like it. As he wrote his wife from Nova Scotia on August 18, 1922, "I would gladly become a vagabond myself and often feel that I'd like to do nothing the rest of my life but sketch and paint and study nature outdoors. I *loathe* school and the thoughts of teaching. I like the lonely shore and the sound of the waves and the little spruce trees and the terns chipping and scolding. But I have no doubt I'll be a very good little boy and join properly in the lockstep when I come back to my prison."

To relax from his tensions as a teacher, MacDonald went sketching during the summer to Coboconk in the Haliburton region of Ontario, or to Lake Simcoe, north of Toronto. He never returned to Algoma after 1920, and for the next few years his sketching trips were less demanding. He combined them with visits to old friends. At Coboconk, he stayed with a former fellow-worker at Grip Limited, Fred Peel, who owned a lumber mill and cottage in the area. For several years, before and after Algoma, MacDonald made regular trips there. At Lake Simcoe, the MacDonalds would visit a cottage at Roches Point owned by Mr. and Mrs. William Hamilton.

Only a few canvases resulted from MacDonald's trips to Coboconk, including Cattle By the Creek of 1918 and River Pastures, Gull River of 1922. It is serene country compared to Algoma, and his paintings of the district reflect it, but it did provide him with the relaxation he needed. On July 3, 1921, he wrote from Coboconk to his son, Thoreau, "I don't suppose you know who won the prize fight. If you do and think it will moderate the heat for us wire us the news. …It is sizzling here – if it wasn't for Little Turtle Lake, so placid out beyond the kitchen door, we might wonder whether 'touristin' is wise or not. …Sketching is not being done by yours truly. Too warm and the landscape not compelling enough to beat the heat, but I think I'd like

Mountains Trees and Sunshine

it here in the Fall instead of Algoma. How'd you like to camp for a couple of weeks late in September?"

In July 1922, after his first full year at the Ontario College of Art, MacDonald visited his life-long artist friend, Lewis Smith, at Petite Rivière, Nova Scotia. He did a considerable number of sketches during more than a month-long stay, and he revived the old love of the sea he had acquired as a youth in England. "It is fine to see the harbour," he wrote to Thoreau in July en route from Saint John, New Brunswick. "It gave me an old time feeling such as I used to have when I would see the ship masts in the river at Newcastle."

On August 4, he wrote his wife, "You remember old Walt Whitman's account of the Long Island shore? This reminds me of it. ...The waves have been magnificent the last days, such a thundering crash and roll – the rattle of the pebbles in the backwash of the waves. And the whole place is so solitary, like Crusoe's coast, so that you almost resent a footprint in the sand. ...I have been attempting to sketch the waves but find this very difficult. Their forms are so variable, the light and colour unapproachable, but they surely make me long to be a marine painter. ...There ought to be a heroic subject there, but I have not seen it complete yet."

MacDonald spent his time at Petite Rivière going to local picnics and children's plays, attending Buck Jones westerns at the local Classic Theatre, and sketching, usually alone, but sometimes with his friends, Lewis and Edith Smith. Unlike his Algoma period, he was unsure of his creative results. "I have made a good many sketches," he wrote. "How they stand I cannot say until I get them home, but they are *different* certainly. I may become something of a marine painter in addition to my other noted accomplishments. There is no doubt whatever that the Atlantic shore is superior to Lake Simcoe as a sketching ground."

MacDonald enlarged only four of his Nova Scotia sketches into canvases, the most important being *Seashore, Nova Scotia* [The National Gallery of Canada] of 1923 and *Church by the Sea* [Vancouver Art Gallery] of 1924. Both of these are very serene compositions, with only incidental movement. The paint surface, particularly in Seashore, Nova Scotia, is almost flat, and there is a very restrained, stylized air about both paintings. It seems as though the never very strong MacDonald was spent by his work on the heroic Algoma canvases and needed a period of creative calm. The passion that burned in the Algoma paintings never quite returned, and was replaced by a more deliberate, design-conscious period. It may have been his search for calm that took the artist in 1924 on his first trip to the Rocky Mountains.

MacDonald certainly found peace and joy in the Rockies. He made seven trips to the mountains, each August from 1924 to 1930, and his affection for them grew with acquaintance. On September 4, 1928, he wrote, "If it is possible to make reservations in Heaven, I am going to have an upper berth somewhere in the O'Hara ranges of Paradise."

On his first trip, MacDonald spent nineteen days in the Rockies, based at Lake O'Hara. It was enough to make him an immediate convert. He wrote home to his wife, thanking her for encouraging him to go there. [Later, on the 1926 mountain trip, she was to accompany him.] Despite his immediate enthusiasm, however, it took MacDonald a while to use the mountains as subject matter for painting. Forms, atmosphere, colour were all new, and a source of constant surprise to him. His palette changed to accommodate the new hues, so different from September in Algoma. As always, MacDonald was eager to share his new-found mountain wonders with others. During his first stay, he wrote his usual numerous letters home, and when he returned to Toronto in early September he almost immediately sat down to write an essay about his journey for the November 1924, issue of *The Bookman*. The article, "A Glimpse of the West", is a long paean to the mountains and prairies.

MacDonald was a passionate believer in a united Canada, and any idea of separatism would have been abhorrent to him, as it would have been to any member of the Group of Seven. For them, the country was one wide canvas and most of them came to know it intimately from coast to coast. Thus, in his *Bookman* article, MacDonald urges, "If I could, I would send every Canadian east of Sault Ste. Marie to the West as a post-graduate course in patriotism." MacDonald was also an ardent conservationist, as he adds, "Thank the red gods we shall always have a background of such things [National Parks]; we cannot plough or pave the whole country, and if our ploughing and paving leave us with a wholesome appetite for the wild, they will be all the wiser done."

Despite the monumental forms of the peaks of O'Hara, Lefroy, Cathedral, Huber, Odoray and others, it was the new colours that intrigued MacDonald from the beginning, "I got to the beautiful O'Hara lying in a rainbow sleep, under the steeps of Mount Lefroy, and the waterfalls of Oesa. And there I realized some of the blessedness of mortals. We may reach our Happy Hunting Grounds and return again, if we take the right train. For nineteen days I wandered in the neighborhood of O'Hara. I sat and sketched her beauty. I looked at the emerald and violet of her colour. It is emerald and malachite, and jade, and rainbow green, and mermaid's eyes, and the beads of Saint Bridget, and the jewels of Patrick's crown, and anything else that the delighted imagination can ascribe to it. ...Rainbow-green seems to me the best. It has a soft quality of light

Lake O'Hara

Cathedral Mountain, Lake O'Hara

and change and variation of intensity which comes the nearest to the feeling of the mountain lake colour."

Although only a few years separate them, MacDonald's Rocky Mountain and Algoma pictures are dramatically different. The rich textures and compositional movement of Algoma are replaced by a generally smooth, almost flat, paint surface. And the deep, resonant colours of Algoma are muted in the mountain canvases to a palette dominated by soft blues, greens and greys. This change is more than one dictated by theme; it represents a fresh approach to picture-making for MacDonald. In his mountainscapes he is concerned with flat divisions of spacial design in a conscious way rarely seen in his earlier work. There is a deliberate, hard-edged clarity evident which may, in part, reflect the fact that he was engaged on a number of large architectural design projects during the mountain period.

The first, and most ambitious of MacDonald's Rocky Mountain paintings, *Rain in the Mountains* [Art Gallery of Hamilton], established the character of his western canvases from the outset. It is the most stylized of all the artist's works. Its planes are as flattened as those in any contemporary "pop" painting. Only in the immediate foreground is there any suggestion of impasto or concern with the modelling of form. Despite the painting's large 48 x 60 inch dimensions, the complex landscape forms it represents are reduced to the barest pictorial minimum. In spite of its title, Rain in the Mountains suggests almost total stillness in its rendering and design. The narrow, neatly delineated shafts of reflections and shoreline are motionless; there is not a ripple in the water; the wraith of mist is frozen in its contours, and the bank of distant rain seems miraculously held in abeyance. This canvas fails to achieve the high visual drama of the best Algoma works, but it is decorative painting of a high order.

Although he made his last trip to the Rockies in August 1930, MacDonald continued to paint mountain themes until his death in 1932. Over an eight-year span, his more than twenty western canvases grew in chromatic subtlety until they became almost pastel in tone. This is evident in two of his very last paintings, *Goat Range, Rocky Mountains* [McMichael Canadian Collection] and *Mountain Snowfall, Lake Oessa* [C.S.Band Estate Collection]. These works, identical in size, are both very restrained in hue, yet manage to convey very contrasting impressions of the mountains. Goat Range is a fairly straightforward portrait of those vast looming masses of rock and glacier. It realistically represents a warm, sunlit August day, with the background range slightly misted over by the late summer haze. Compositionally, the picture is

Stopping the Tempest

almost divided in two diagonally between the dark foreground range and the lighter peaks beyond. Compared to the more reportorial Goat Range, Mountain Snowfall is a lyric work which graphically unites the painter and the poet in MacDonald. Its delicacy of design perfectly portrays the silence of the falling snow. Here, MacDonald closes in on a detail of the Rockies, turning its white, linear accents of snow banks into a near-abstract pattern against the pearl-grey background of the mountainside.

MacDonald's affection for the Rockies produced very different images from the Rockwell Kent inspired stark blue and white cones of Lawren Harris. MacDonald's creative character was not the kind that imposes its forms upon nature, to subdue her, but rather elicits from her its responses of the moment. Thus, each of his paintings of the mountains is somewhat different in viewpoint and in style. None of his mountain pictures equals in power his masterpieces of northern Ontario, but they nevertheless compose a rich pictorial lode from one of the most difficult and forbidding of all landscape subjects.

In early 1923, MacDonald received the most important design commission of his career, when he was appointed designer for the decorations of St. Anne's Anglican Church on Gladstone Avenue in Toronto. It was an assignment for which he had been waiting for fifteen years. When St. Anne's was first opened in 1908, its rector, Lawrence Skey, discussed with MacDonald his ambition to decorate his church in the Byzantine tradition of its architecture. MacDonald was eager to undertake the job, but it was a decade and a half before funds became available to underwrite its costs, after a parishioner, Samuel Stewart, left five thousand dollars in his will for the purpose and the congregation raised an additional five thousand dollars.

MacDonald worked closely with architect William Rae in the decoration of St. Anne's. Canon Skey explained, "We decided to select the artist and architect whose combined ability would be the most likely to produce a colour scheme which would be reverent, harmonious and in keeping with the architecture of the church." MacDonald, for his part, confessed, "It was the first big decoration job I had done. It was indeed an act of faith on Mr. Skey's part." From April to July of 1923, MacDonald applied himself to a study of Byzantine art at the University of Toronto library, in preparation for his layout of the church walls and its huge dome which had a diameter of fifty-five feet. By the end of July, he had completed his small, rough concepts for each of the twenty-one panels which were to be incorporated.

"There were things that struck me in studying the Byzantine empire," noted MacDonald.

"I am convinced more and more that we don't advance very much in art and thought. Things just seem to go up and down. We don't change much. Some of the books on art I had to read were written twenty-five years ago. The old-masters they pooh-poohed as painting sunk to its lowest degradation are held up by Clive Bell and other critics today as the very finest things in art."

MacDonald never intended to carry out the total decorating scheme for St. Anne's by himself. He originally wanted to use Ontario College of Art students to enlarge his compositions. "It was to be," he said, "a sort of community job. I've always had the idea that this would be a good way to work, not one individual getting the credit, but all working together, sharing the result. I should like to have had the students, but most of them go away in the summertime and, for that reason, it was impossible. So the work was done by other artists in Toronto, who gladly cooperated with me, to whom I sublet the contracts."

The loss of the students was probably St. Anne's gain, for among the twelve artists employed in its decoration were some of the most gifted painters, designers and sculptors in the country. They included two of MacDonald's Group of Seven colleagues, F.H.Varley and Franklin Carmichael, the sculptors Francis Loring and Florence Wyle, as well as Herbert Palmer, Thoreau MacDonald, Arthur Martin [MacDonald's old colleague at the Carlton Studio], Neil McKechnie, Herbert Stansfield, James Blomfield and John Keeley.

MacDonald chose for himself the panels representing *The Tempest, The Crucifixion* and *The Transfiguration*. Like all the paintings for the church, these were executed in a flat, shadowless style, in a modern adaptation of the Byzantine manner. The largest panels in the scheme are the triangle-shaped pendentives in the dome, which measure ten by fifteen feet and include MacDonald's Crucifixion and F.H.Varley's The Nativity. Among the other major paintings are Carmichael's Adoration of the Magi and Entry into Jerusalem.

MacDonald explained his concept for St. Anne's in an article for the May-June issue of the *Journal of the Royal Architectural Institute of Canada.* "It was decided that the religious feeling of the people of St. Anne's would be best expressed by combining the flat treatment and strong colouring of the Byzantine style with the completer illustrative quality of later work down to Giotto. ...The work was done cooperatively but independently, all the associated artists working in their own studios, from small scale designs prepared by the decorating contractor [Mac-Donald], keeping their work in close harmony with the general design, using the same strength

The Transfiguration

of colour throughout, and drawing on a common stock of materials for their supplies. A limited number of colours were used, and combined or reduced they gave a great variety, but the same colour in the same tonality appears somewhere in each decoration. The colours were a crimson red, venetian red, yellow ochre, ultramarine blue, permanent green, black, umber and ivory white."

MacDonald modestly refused to make any great claims for the St. Anne's project, although it remains one of the most successful ever achieved in Canada. "No one," he wrote, "who had anything to do with the work, remembering the standards of Giotto and Ravenna, would claim any great artistic merit for it. But it was a local effort, honestly and enthusiastically made, by a congregation modest in means and ritual."

When asked why he had chosen MacDonald as decorator for his church, Canon Skey replied, "I chose MacDonald because he was a truly religious man, even if he doesn't go to church." MacDonald was not a church-going man. Nor was he ever, as has often been stated, a member of the Presbyterian faith. [Perhaps his Scottish name misled people in this respect; even A.Y.Jackson mistakenly called him "a Presbyterian interested in Christian Science."] As a young man, he was an Anglican, but he left that church permanently at the end of August 1896, at the age of twenty-three. MacDonald tolerated his wife's ardent adherence to the Christian Science Church, but he never joined it, even in the most informal way. When asked to what faith he did belong, he often replied, half-jesting, "the Arts and Letters Club" or, more seriously, "the brotherhood of man". Although he resigned from the Anglican Church, MacDonald remained a Christian, with a strong touch of Pantheism, throughout his life.

In the same year as St. Anne's project, MacDonald won the Royal Canadian Academy's competition for an interior mural design with his *A Friendly Meeting, Early Canada*, which incorporated Indian, priest and explorer. [F.H.Varley was the runner-up in the competition.] But MacDonald had to wait five years for another architectural design commission. During the summer of 1928, he planned the decorative scheme for the moorish-style lounge of the Claridge Apartment Building in Toronto. It was a very modest venture compared to St. Anne's, but its simple, art-deco design has retained its vitality over half-a-century. It incorporates the signs of the zodiac and a series of banded patterns in the ceiling beams. It is highly geometric in concept and bright in colour, featuring red, blue and gold on a cream ground. The actual execution of the Claridge interior was carried out by his former student, Carl Schaefer, in the early fall of 1928, while MacDonald was painting in the mountains.

MacDonald's final architectural project, for Toronto's downtown Concourse Building, was also carried out in 1928. The nineteen-storey building, which opened in February 1929, was an architectural landmark of its period. MacDonald was so enthusiastic about the building that he wrote a long article, "City of Future Brilliant With Gold and Colour", about it in the Toronto *Telegram* of February 26, 1929, in which he makes the visionary statement: "The Colour Age seems to have some interesting possibilities, and it looks as though our architects and their clients are about to enjoy themselves. There seems to be no reason why business and building should not be entertaining as well as efficient."

The front entrance of the Concourse Building was decorated with a large panel in mosaic, representing in symbolic form the elements of air, fire, earth and water. The theme was suggested, explained MacDonald, "by the name Concourse, a gathering together". The ceiling of the interior foyer was ornamented by national wildlife motifs of deer, Canadian trees and flowers, wild ducks and sporting fish in gold and brilliant colours. Quotes from eight Canadian poets were incorporated into the designs. The mosaics were carried out by two Italian craftsmen under MacDonald's direct supervision. Thoreau MacDonald designed seven small entrance panels and Carl Schaefer carried out all of the painting of the interior decorations.

In 1930, MacDonald made his last trip to his beloved Rockies. He stayed at Lake O'Hara Bungalow Camp from August 29 to September 17. On that last journey westward, he wrote Thoreau a letter from west of Regina, August 28, in which he continued his lifelong habit of making verbal landscape notes from trains: "The whole world has been prairie, sky and all. We began with showers east of Winnipeg and even a rainbow soon after sunrise – something special in raising the curtain, then we got fine breaks of sunshine with the Manitoba maples all dripping with rain, and that weather moving off to the north where it lay along the horizon like a great grey blanket thrown off the bed. ...This has been the prairie at its best, wonderful expanse and clear, simple colour and straight line composition all through. You would like it, I'm sure. Many of the smaller sloughs are dried up, but the ducks are making the most of what is left, a little crowded in places, but quite happy. The sun has gone flaming and burning into the great rounded slopes as we wait, and the cool moon is in the south. We are in the rolling prairie now, and it goes back and back in a thick folded loneliness very impressive to see." MacDonald was devoted to trains, and his journeys on them composed an important part of his painting trips. He enjoyed the people he met on board, particularly children, and his letters are full of humorous observations about the transient human comedy.

Although he painted five known canvases in 1930, MacDonald produced no new canvases

Breezy Shore

during 1931, although he retouched the 1922 Algoma painting, Northland Hilltop during that year. The demands of his role as principal of the Ontario College of Art seem to have been especially heavy during 1931, although MacDonald did manage a sketching trip to McGregor Bay in early September. But it was clear that MacDonald's limited strengths were being taxed, and in November, shortly after being elected a full member of the Royal Canadian Academy, he had a mild stroke. He was bedridden for several weeks, and late the following January took a leave of absence from the Art College to recuperate in the Barbados. He sailed with his wife from Boston early in February and did not return to Toronto until the seventh of May.

While in the West Indies, MacDonald was impressed by the flowers and vegetation and the brilliant white light. He painted a considerable number of Barbados sketches, of a higher key than anything he had previously done. Most of these are of a more casual character than the majority of his Canadian sketches, but they prove, once again, MacDonald's ability to quickly adjust to a new landscape environment. The subject matter of the three-month southern period is mostly of the sea coast, with a few close-up studies of flowers.

As on other trips, MacDonald was reluctant to return to the Art College. He was never really suited to a position of administration, though it put food on his table. And in the Barbados, as in Nova Scotia, he luxuriated in the sense of freedom he always found by the sea. After he returned home, he wrote to a Barbadian friend on May 13, 1932, "Dear Miss Louie – I am just beginning to wake up though we have been home a week. The weather has been quite dull, cold, grey and rainy, and our little Barbadian souls have drawn within themselves to think about the far away brightness of the blessed island. ...By the time you get this you will have many frangipanis and flamboyants, not to mention roses and verbenas and, of course, you can always beat us in sunshine and skies. As we came northwards, it was like climbing the steps of spring, warmest and brightest south, colder and more reticent north. ...before we got to Boston, all the overcoats and fur collars seemed as light as a bathing suit in Bathsheba."

Despite his recent illness, MacDonald immediately returned to some of his Art College duties. "The College of Art is just closing," he reported in May. "I am to take a little part in the final exercises tonight. The College has had many troubles, and much illness among the students this winter, but has come through very nicely. I am hoping to take on some light administrative work after the students leave. There are certain problems of readjustment and continuance to be taken up and I am to have the staff to lunch on Saturday."

MacDonald's determination to return to work immediately may have hastened his early death. During 1932, he painted six canvases as well as directing the Ontario College of Art. Early in the school year, on November 22, he suffered a massive stroke in his office at the College. He was taken to his Duggan Avenue home by his friend, Dr. Frederick Banting and a Dr. Cameron. He never regained consciousness and died four days later, on November 26, 1932.

J.E.H.MacDonald was buried in a family plot in Toronto's Prospect Cemetery, under a simple marker bearing his initials and his dates. There is no epitaph, but a fitting one might be found in his own poem, "Autumn Sunflowers":

Here in the garden corner
What holy rite is done,
Between the breeze and branches
The sunflowers and the sun.

I sit beside the service
In which the flowers bend,
Their lowly rapture holds me
To listen to the end.

I thought a sadness pending
The stooping flowers told,
Of summer downward wending
Brooding withdrawn and old.

In the celestial moment
Nor past nor present runs,
And thought and earth and body
Are flaming of the sun.

Lake Simcoe, c 1921

Bridge at Petite Riviere, Nova Scotia, c 1922

J.E.H. MacDonald '22

Old Dock, Petite Riviere, Nova Scotia, 1922

Nova Scotian Shore, 1922

Windy Day, Little Turtle Lake, 1922

Buckwheat Field, 1923

In a Wheat Field: Evening Shadows, 1929

Rain in the Mountains, c 1924

Dark Autumn, Rocky Mountains, 1930

Lake O'Hara, Rainy Weather, 1928

Clearing Weather, Sherbrooke Lake, above Wapta Lake, c 1930

Rain, Wiwaxy Peaks, Lake O'Hara, c 1930

Snow, Lake O'Hara Camp, 1927

Lake McArthur, c 1925

Mountain and Larches, Rocky Mountains, c 1930

Mountain Stream, Opabin Pass, 1929

Mount Ordray, 1930

Near Lake Oessa, Abbot's Pass, 1930

September Snow on Mount Schaffer, c 1929

Lake O'Hara, c 1930

Lake McArthur, Yoho Park, 1924

Hazy Day Ordray, c 1930

Lichen Covered Shale Slabs, 1930

Goat Range Rocky Mountains, 1932

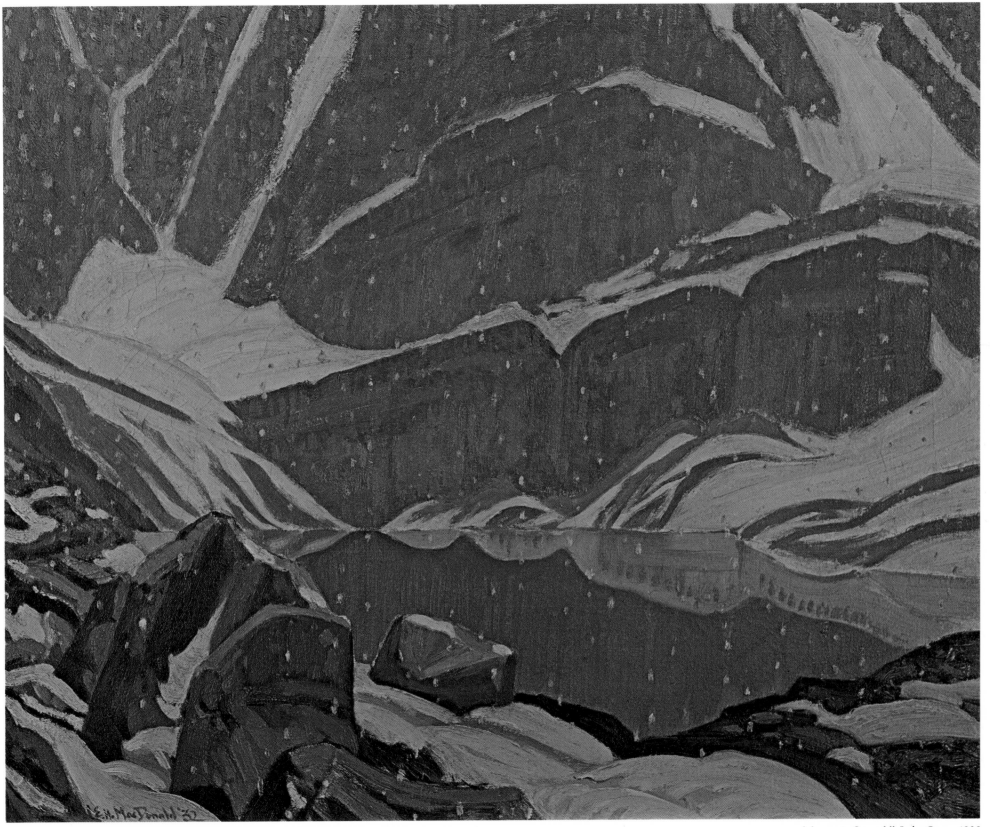

Mountain Snowfall, Lake Oessa, 1932

Little Turtle Lake, 1927

Windy Day, McLeans Island, Sturgeon Bay, 1931

Palms, Barbados, 1932

Barbados, 1932

J.E.H.MacDonald

J.R.Lavis
Bertha MacDonald
Thoreau MacDonald
J.E.H.MacDonald
Joan MacDonald

Mrs. A. Lismer and Daughter
Mrs. J.E.H.MacDonald
Thoreau MacDonald

Thornhill 1916-17

J.E.H.MacDonald, Sturgeon Bay, 1931

J.E.H.MacDonald and F.H.Johnston, Algoma, 1919

Opabin Mountains, September, 1930

Index to the Works

93 Coboconk Village
Brush and Ink Drawing
Private Collection

95 A Sandy Beach, Lake Ontario, 1918
Oil on canvas
40.6 x 50.8 cm (16 x 20″)
Mr. and Mrs. Max Merkur

96 Algoma Woodland, 1918
Oil on board
21.6 x 26.7 cm (8½ x 10½″)
The McMichael Canadian Collection

97 Young Maples, Algoma, 1918
Oil on board
21.6 x 26.7 cm (8½ x 10½″)
The McMichael Canadian Collection

98 The Little Falls, (Sketch), 1918
Oil on board
21.6 x 26.7 cm (8½ x 10½″)
The Art Gallery of Ontario

99 The Little Falls, 1919
Oil on canvas
71.12 x 91.44 cm (28 x 36″)
London Art Gallery

100 Beaver Dam, Algoma, Near Mongoose Lake, 1918
Oil on board
21.6 x 26.7 cm (8½ x 10½″)
The National Gallery of Canada

101 Near Montreal Lake Algoma, 1919
Oil on board
22.2 x 27.3 cm (8¾ x 10¾″)
The National Gallery of Canada

102 Gleams on the Hills, 1918
Oil on board
21.6 x 26.7 cm (8½ x 10½″)
The National Gallery of Canada

103 Algoma (Hill), 1919
Oil on board
21.6 x 26.7 cm (8½ x 10½″)
Mr. and Mrs. W.A.Manford Collection

104 Near Hubert, Algoma, 1919
Oil on board
21.6 x 26.7 cm (8½ x 10½″)
Mr. and Mrs. W.A.Manford Collection

105 Algoma, 1919
Oil on board
21.6 x 26.7 cm (8½ x 10½″)
Mr. and Mrs. W.A.Manford Collection

106 Algoma Bush, September, 1919
Oil on board
21.6 x 26.7 cm (8½ x 10½″)
The McMichael Canadian Collection

107 Lake in the Valley, 1919
Oil on board
21.6 x 26.7 cm (8½ x 10½″)
The McMichael Canadian Collection

108 Beaver Pond, Algoma, c 1919
Oil on board
21.6 x 26.7 cm (8½ x 10½″)
Private Collection

109 Montreal Lake, Algoma, c 1919
Oil on board
21.6 x 26.7 cm (8½ x 10½″)
The National Gallery of Canada

110 Fall Woods, Algoma, c 1919
Oil on board
21.6 x 26.7 cm (8½ x 10½″)
Mr. and Mrs. W.A.Manford Collection

111 Algoma Bush, Autumn, c 1919
Oil on board
21.6 x 26.7 cm (8½ x 10½″)
The National Gallery of Canada

112 Beaver Dam and Birches, 1919
Oil on board
22.6 x 26.7 cm (8⅞ x 10½″)
The McMichael Canadian Collection

113 The Beaver Dam, 1919
Oil on canvas
81.6 x 86.7 cm (32⅛ x 34⅛″)
The Art Gallery of Ontario

114 Leaves in the Brook, 1918
Oil on board
21.6 x 26.7 cm (8½ x 10½″)
The McMichael Canadian Collection

115 Leaves in the Brook, 1919
Oil on canvas
53.3 x 66.0 cm (21 x 26″)
The McMichael Canadian Collection

116 Moose Lake, Algoma, 1919
Oil on board
21.6 x 26.7 cm (8½ x 10½″)
The McMichael Canadian Collection

117 Agawa, 1920
Oil on board
21.6 x 26.7 cm (8½ x 10½″)
The McMichael Canadian Collection

118 Algoma Hills, 1920
Oil on board
21.6 x 26.7 cm (8½ x 10½″)
The McMichael Canadian Collection

119 Algoma, c 1920
Oil on board
21.6 x 26.7 cm (8½ x 10½″)
The National Gallery of Canada

120 Sungleams, Algoma Hilltop, 1920
Oil on board
21.6 x 26.7 cm (8½ x 10½″)
The McMichael Canadian Collection

121 Silver Swamp, Algoma, 1919
Oil on board
21.6 x 26.7 cm (8½ x 10½″)
The McMichael Canadian Collection

122 Solemn Land, c 1918-19
Oil on board
21.6 x 26.7 cm (8½ x 10½″)
The Art Gallery of Ontario

123 The Solemn Land, 1921
Oil on canvas
121.9 x 152.4 cm (48 x 60″)
The National Gallery of Canada

162   Lake O'Hara, Rainy Weather, 1928
Oil on board
21.6 x 26.7 cm (8½ x 10½″)
The McMichael Canadian Collection

163   Clearing Weather, Sherbrooke Lake,
above Wapta Lake, c 1930
Oil on board
21.3 x 26.4 cm (8⅜ x 10⅜″)
The National Gallery of Canada

164   Rain, Wiwaxy Peaks, Lake O'Hara, c 1930
Oil on board
21.6 x 26.7 cm (8½ x 10½″)
The National Gallery of Canada

165   Snow, Lake O'Hara Camp, 1927
Oil on board
21.6 x 26.7 cm (8½ x 10½″)
The McMichael Canadian Collection

166   Lake McArthur, c 1925
Oil on board
21.6 x 26.7 cm (8½ x 10½″)
The National Gallery of Canada

167   Mountain and Larches, Rocky Mountain, c 1930
Oil on board
21.6 x 26.7 cm (8½ x 10½″)
The National Gallery of Canada

168   Mountain Stream, Opabin Pass, 1929
Oil on board
21.6 x 26.7 cm (8½ x 10½″)
The National Gallery of Canada

169   Mount Ordray, 1930
Oil on board
21.6 x 26.7 cm (8½ x 10½″)
The National Gallery of Canada

170   Near Lake Oessa, Abott's Pass, 1930
Oil on board
21.6 x 26.7 cm (8½ x 10½″)
The National Gallery of Canada

171   September Snow on Mount Schaffer, c 1929
Oil on board
21.6 x 26.7 cm (8½ x 10½″)
The National Gallery of Canada

172   Lake O'Hara, c 1930
Oil on board
21.6 x 26.7 cm (8½ x 10½″)
The National Gallery of Canada

173   Lake McArthur, Yoho Park, 1924
Oil on board
22.2 x 26.4 cm (8¾ x 10⅜″)
The National Gallery of Canada

174   Hazy Day Ordray, c 1930
Oil on board
21.6 x 26.7 cm (8½ x 10½″)
Mr. and Mrs.W.A.Manford Collection

175   Lichen Covered Shale Slabs, 1930
Oil on board
21.6 x 26.7 cm (8½ x 10½″)
The McMichael Canadian Collection

176   Goat Range Rocky Mountains, 1932
Oil on canvas
53.3 x 66 cm (21 x 26″)
The McMichael Canadian Collection

177   Mountain Snow Fall, Lake Oessa, 1932
Oil on canvas
53.3 x 66 cm (21 x 26″)
C.S.Band Estate Collection

178   Little Turtle Lake, 1927
Oil on board
13.3 x 21.6 cm (5¼ x 8½″)
The McMichael Canadian Collection

179   Windy Day, McLeans Island, Sturgeon Bay, 1931
Oil on board
21.6 x 26.7 cm (8½ x 10½″)
Art Gallery of Hamilton

180   Palms, Barbados, 1932
Oil on board
21.6 x 26.7 cm (8½ x 10½″)
The Art Gallery of Ontario

181   Barbados, 1932
Oil on board
21.6 x 26.7 cm (8½ x 10½″)
The Art Gallery of Ontario

183   J.E.H.MacDonald

184   Family Portrait
Thornhill, 1916-17

185   J.E.H.MacDonald, Sturgeon Bay, 1931
J.E.H.MacDonald and F.H.Johnston, Algoma, 1919

186   J.E.H.MacDonald, Opabin Mountains, September, 1930

THE TANGLED GARDEN

Design and Production: V. JOHN LEE, Toronto, Ontario
Photography: T. E. MOORE, Toronto, Ontario
Typesetting: THE HOUSE OF LIND, Toronto, Ontario
Colour Separation and Film Assembly: FACSIMILE PLUS, Markham, Ontario
Platemaking and Printing: ASHTON POTTER, Toronto, Ontario

This book is dedicated to the Canadian Craftsman;
who understand the value of painstaking attention
to detail

Publishing Concept: Bernard Loates

Additional photographs by: The National Gallery of Canada,
The McMichael Canadian Collection, The Art Gallery of Ontario,
The London Art Gallery and the Saskatoon Art Gallery.